Hablot Knight Browne

All about kisses

Hablot Knight Browne

All about kisses

ISBN/EAN: 9783741172090

Manufactured in Europe, USA, Canada, Australia, Japa

Cover: Foto ©Andreas Hilbeck / pixelio.de

Manufactured and distributed by brebook publishing software (www.brebook.com)

Hablot Knight Browne

All about kisses

ALL ABOUT KISSES.

BY

DAMOCLES.

WITH ONE HUNDRED ILLUSTRATIONS
BY
HABLOTT K. BROWN,
(PHIZ).

LONDON:
CHARLES HENRY CLARKE,
13, PATERNOSTER ROW, E.C.

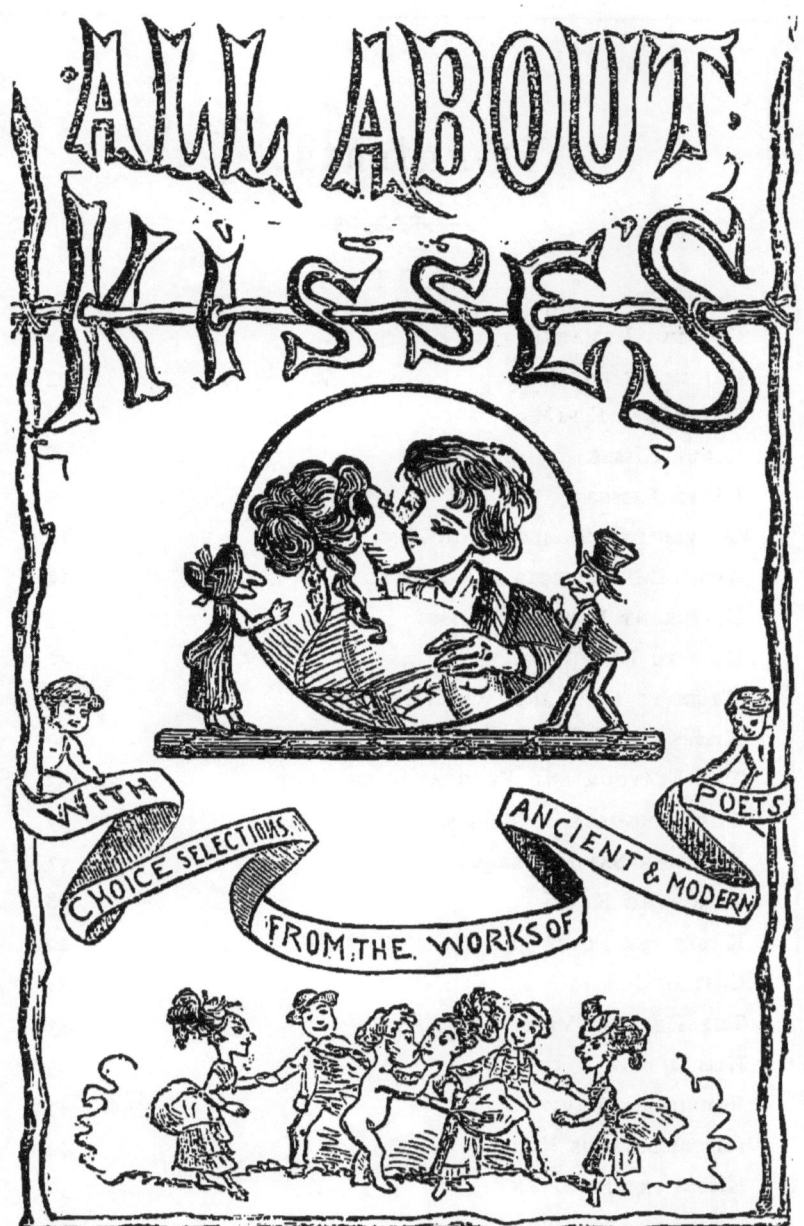

Contents.

PART I.

	PAGE
OPENING REMARKS	1
ORIGIN OF THE KISS	3
WHAT IS A KISS?	4
EARLY KISSES	6
LATER KISSES	9
CONVENIENT SUBJECTS FOR KISSING	11
AWKWARD SUBJECTS FOR KISSING	14
DIFFERENT KINDS OF KISSES	17
HOW TO KISS	22
WHEN TO KISS, AND WHEN NOT	26
KISSES IN COURTSHIP	29
THE FLAVOUR AND FRAGRANCE OF KISSES	33
THE LANGUAGE OF KISSES	37
FAMILIAR SAYINGS ABOUT KISSES	37
THROWING KISSES	38
KISSES PER POST	40
COST OF KISSES	41
THE HEALING VIRTUE OF KISSES	43
KISS IN THE RING	45
FORBIDDEN FRUIT	47
MISCELLANEOUS KISSES	49
KISSES IN THE OVEN	50
KISSES IN THE CUP	51

CONTENTS. v

	PAGE
AN EASY WAY OF MAKING GLOVES ...	52
WHIST; KISSING THE DEALER	54
KISSING THE HAND OR FOOT	56
LIPS	60
UNDER THE MISTLETOE	64
KISSES IN SONG ...	67
KISSES AT MARRIAGES ...	69
RUSSIAN AND GERMAN CUSTOMS ...	69
KISSES AND COLDS ...	71
KISSES AND GAPES ...	71
OMNIUM GATHERUM ...	73

PART II.

(SELECTIONS FROM)

BYRON, LORD ...	103
BURNS ...	121
BONNEFONS, JEAN ...	192
BONFADIUS ...	220
BAIF ...	220
BUCHANAN	221
BEAUMONT AND FLETCHER ...	143
CANNAZAR	208
COLERIDGE ...	133
COMBE	136
DRUMMOND	142
FONTANUS ...	217

CONTENTS.

	PAGE
GALLUS	219
GARRICK	156
GUARINI	224
HOOD, TOM	138
HUNT, LEIGH	141
HORACE	206
HILL, AARON	158
JONSON, BEN	145
KEATS	153
MOORE, TOM	108
MURET	217
MARTIAL	228
OVID	209
PINDAR, PETER	149
PASQUIER	227
PLATO	227
SHAKESPEARE	87
SECUNDUS, JOHANNES	175
SHELLEY	155
SAPPHO	224
STEPHENS	147
STANLEY	139
TENNYSON	126
WHITE, KIRKE	154
VARIOUS AUTHORS	160

PART I.

Kisses in Prose.

Opening Remarks.

"ALL about Kisses." I can imagine the astonished reader exclaiming, with particular emphasis on the first word—"Bosh! all about fiddlesticks!" Precisely! the reader and I agree. It would be as absurd for me to attempt to tell *all* about kisses as it would be to tell all about those indispensable sticks that lure the sweet music from the fiddle! My attempt is less absurd; my aim less presumptuous. If the reader will remove the emphasis from "all," and put it on the "kisses," it will better suit "my book," and give greater satisfaction to the person operated upon.

If kissing is not a science, it may certainly be considered a Fine Art. It has been practised and promulgated in all countries and in all ages, but in no country has it found more zealous devotees, or more of them, than in England, and yet one would be puzzled to rake up half-a-dozen printed works on the subject! The knowledge of the art has been principally conveyed from mouth to mouth.

To supply a long-felt want (?), this little volume on kisses and kissing is offered. I do not claim for it literary merit, nor yet the reader's *serious* perusal of its pages. My effort has been to make it as entertaining and useful as possible. In the advice and observations put forth, I have addressed myself more particularly to *man*, as he stands most in need of the same. It is for *man* to kiss, and for *woman* to be kissed. There is no law, however, against woman kissing, nor could such a law be desired.

In this little labour of love I have availed myself of the assistance of many famous authors, ancient and modern. The text will be illustrated with numerous grotesque sketches from my own pencil, which, I hope, may provoke an occasional smile or hearty laugh.

THE AUTHOR.

Brighton.

Origin of the Kiss.

THE origin of the kiss, like the origin of many other things, is involved in obscurity. It is not our intention to clear up the mystery—in fact, we can't. Our first parents very likely knew something of the matter. It is not unreasonable to suppose that Adam bestowed many a loving kiss on his fair partner, and that she kissed him in return. We are strengthened in the belief that it was so by the fact that kisses have about them so much of the ambrosial sweetness, that, in our ideas, we associate with an earthly paradise.

The first kiss on record is the one Jacob gave to Rachel, on meeting her at the well; the second is that given to Jacob by Rachel's father. We are not told which kiss Jacob liked best! They were both model kisses—the first was a kiss of love, and the second a kiss of peace—a Christian salute. The ancients cultivated both kinds of kisses; but in modern times the kiss of peace has fallen into disuse, especially among men; the women occasionally use it among themselves, but there is more formality than meaning about it. We now rely entirely on the kiss of love, which, of course, is capable of many degrees of expression and application. It answers every purpose for which a kiss is required.

What is a Kiss?

EVERYBODY knows what a kiss is. The blushing maiden of sweet seventeen knows; that roguish twinkle in her eye tells us that she has often had one. The school-boy knows what a kiss is, and so does the schoolgirl. The old people know quite well, and even the baby knows. The rich and poor, old and young, all know, and could show us what a kiss is—even make us feel its meaning, but could either of them *tell* us? Let Edwin ask his Angelina what a kiss is, and if she does not evade the question, and call him something or other, it will be odd, and even worth entering in his diary, if he is thoughtless enough to keep one! A kiss is one of those things more easily felt than described. Josh Billings says, "The more a man tries to analyse a kiss, the more he can't. Any man who can sit down, tilt his chair back, place his feet on the mantel-piece, and tell how a kiss tastes, has no more real flavour in his mouth than a knot-hole. The only way to define a kiss is to take one." There happens to be much truth in the foregoing observations. A soldier once attempted to define a kiss, and so far succeeded as to say that it was "a report at head-quarters." A civilian also tried, but signally failed. He must have been spooney. "A kiss," said he, "is a receipt given you by a lady, on paying your addresses!" That is a very one-sided and exclusive definition.

Referring to my old and learned friend, Dr. Johnson, who has helped me, as he has many others, out of frequent wordy difficulties, I find that even he shirks the responsibility of defining the word, but gives the definition of Dryden, and this is it:—

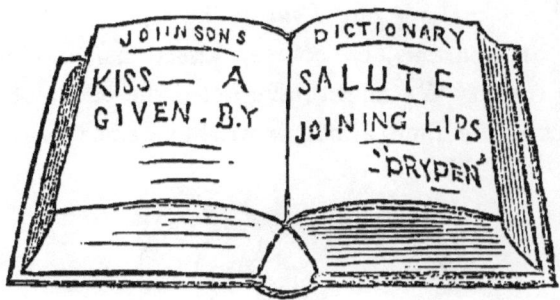

Eureka! we need inquire no further. A kiss in Dryden's time, our time, or anyone else's time, was and is the same.

Early Kisses.

A S far back as memory will carry us, and long ere that, we met with kisses. Kisses were about the first things we received after making our *début* in the world. Our doting parents, of course, kissed us, and so did Sairey Gamp. We might have noted the odour of gin in her kiss at the time, although we have since forgotten it.

Before we were many weeks old, all our immediate relations and friends, and many of our distant ones, especially the feminine portion of them, had given us the usual labial salute and passed the usual compliment—"What a fine baby!" Some of them would, perhaps, rather not have kissed us, and, on the other hand, perhaps we had rather they had not, but customs and formalities had to be observed. Kissing was the very first thing we were taught, and it was wonderful how soon we picked up the knowledge; indeed, kissing, like Dogberry's learning, seems to come by nature. When we could kiss, what a time we had! We were called upon to kiss

promiscuously everybody and nearly everything we came in contact with! Our existence was one scene of kissing and being kissed. At no subsequent period of our lives have we been required to endure so much in that way. Some of the kisses we used to get then *were* kisses! We used to dread them! They were positively dangerous. At times we were afraid part of our little cheeks or arms would have been sucked into somebody's mouth and been lost to us for ever. The mouths were so large, as we then thought, and the kisses so vehement. And then, again, what dreadful marks some of them left behind, seldom smaller than a crown-piece, but they soon disappeared. As months passed on, and we grew into years, and could run about, we did not get quite so many kisses as when we were in arms, and that may be accounted for by the fact that we were not then so near to anybody's mouth, and that other claimants had arrived on the scene. But we were not short of kisses even then, we had as many as we wanted, and were satisfied.

> "When I was a little baby,
>   Gals would never let me be,
> For every one would snatch me up
>   And place me on her knee;
> Then so kiss and squeeze and hug me,
>   I'm sure that 'Dad' and 'Mam'
> Must have wondered I surviv'd it,
>   But I stood it like a lamb.

> "And again while but in boyhood,
>   They'd tempt me from my home,
> Through gardens and through pleasure grounds,
>   O'er fairy spots to roam;
> Then with luscious fruits and sweetmeats
>   My small 'tummy' they would cram,
> And half stifle me with kisses,
>   But I stood it like a lamb."

Later Kisses.

THE first time in our lives when we are likely to run short of kisses is when we are in our teens. A certain French writer describes young ladies as creatures that cease to kiss gentlemen at twelve, and begin again at twenty! He might have said something of the same

sort about young gentlemen. At the period referred to however, the kisses that are lacking in quantity are more than compensated for in quality, for, despite what the French writer says, there *are* kisses. Early kisses are insipid—in fact, nothing better than mere mechanical salutes, those of later years are tasty, full of meaning and feeling—spiritual. One of them goes a long way, and we have often to go a long way for it, and it is well that it is so. It would not do for us to indulge in the art to the extent that we did in our younger days. It would unfit us for the affairs of daily life. We happen to live in prosaic times, and work that we may eat. If we lived in some happy region where labour was unknown, we might devote ourselves to the luxurious indulgence of kissing, without, perhaps, being much the worse for it. As it is, we must be contented with an occasional kiss, and, bringing our practical experience to bear upon it, extract the greatest possible amount of bliss therefrom—then wait till fortune favours us with the next—not forgetting the Latin motto,

"Audaces Fortuna Juvat."

Convenient Subjects for Kissing.

JUST as some subjects are awkward for kissing, others are very convenient, that is, there are no physical, although there may be moral, difficulties in the way. A prominent nose is a great difficulty, and not easily surmounted, but a prominent lip is quite the reverse. The

flatter the nose and the more prominent the lips, the easier the kissing. It is an acknowledged fact that too frequent kissing has a tendency to blunt the nose and draw out the lips. Be careful, therefore, that while you are indulging in kisses, you don't at the same time spoil the beauty of your face.

On the preceding page are a few examples of what might be considered convenient subjects for kissing.

Mark the young gentleman at the top, and the lady on either side. Are not their lips well located? The noses differ, but that is of no consequence, they are out of the way of the mouths, and so will not interfere with the kisses. Good, kind noses! Would that they were more general!

Looking at the young lady at the bottom, who is not constrained to exclaim with Ovid—

> "Short is her mouth, her lips are made to kiss,
> Rosy and full, and prodigal of bliss."

Or with our own great poet, Shakespeare—

> "O how ripe in show
> Thy lips, those kissing cherries tempting grow."

And what can be said of the young gentleman facing her. His nose will never interfere with his kissing—it is too far away from his mouth to be guilty of such a thing.

A moderate-sized, or small mouth is better for kissing than a large one. If the mouth is too large, there is a danger of the kiss slipping in instead of resting on the lips, and, on the other hand, if the mouth is too small, it will not be possible to make with the lips a nice-sized kiss, such as a lover would prefer, although it might be just the thing for a child. A slight moustache on a gentleman's lip is no objection, but very objectionable on a lady's.

Awkward Subjects for Kissing.

GENERALLY speaking, kissing is *easy* work, that is if you have a subject to operate upon. The *difficulty* is to find a subject. Now and then, thank goodness, it is not oftener, an uncommonly awkward subject turns up, one that was either never meant for kissing or had been

spoilt by age, neglect, or some other cause. Kissing is quite out of the question, even if it were possible, it would never be worth the trouble. Our illustration supplies a few examples of what might be considered awkward subjects for kissing.

The old lady at the top, it is to be hoped, has seen better days, and creditably passed through a kissing career ere her nose and chin attempted to shake hands, and for ever spoilt her mouth for the art. But what can be said of the younger subjects? Note the leading feature of the gentleman to the right, and the lady to the left. Nature, when endowing them so lavishly with noses, perchance forgot that mouths were used for other purposes than feeding! These are two very distressing cases. There is only one remedy, and that is a desperate one—to excise the obstructive members, and trust to Nature to supply better ones!

Of the two remaining awkward subjects, the lady is the most unfortunate. Her lips will persist in keeping so far apart, and exposing the teeth. It would not be a bad mouth for kissing if the lips could be drawn together. The gentleman's lips are invisible and inaccessible by reason of the hirsute ornament under his nose. If you made the attempt you would only kiss his hair, and if you made an attempt with the lady, you would only kiss her teeth! The gentleman certainly has the advantage. Whenever he feels disposed to "go in" for kisses, it is in his power to remove the great obstacle in a very few minutes by the friendly aid of a pair of scissors and a razor. It is a noteworthy fact that gentlemen of this stamp invariable take it into their heads, at some time or other, to have a "clean shave." The motive is unquestionably laudable.

The labial salute is not easily given when a convenient subject meets with an awkward one, but when two awkward ones come together, what then!

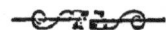

Different kinds of Kisses.

KISSES are of great variety. They differ in size, strength, duration, taste, feeling, &c. They are good, bad, or indifferent. There are three sizes—small, medium, and large.

The "Suaviolum," or small kiss, is made by children, and persons with very small mouths, or by persons with ordinary mouths, when a ceremonial kiss is required. It is also used much for stage purposes, as there is little actual meaning in it.

> "The kiss, it is true,
> For children may do,
> The passionless, aged, or grave."

but it is no good to the lover—he requires a more sub-

stantial kiss, and a worthier exponent of his feelings.

The large or "slobbering" kiss is the small kiss in its most exaggerated form! One is undeveloped and the other is over-developed. It is generally made by vulgar people. It is a well-meant kiss, although not unlike a playful bite. A pocket-handkerchief should be in readiness to wipe the place! It covers too much space, and makes too much noise. It is appreciated by those who like quantity.

The Medium or "Love" kiss is the perfect one, and the one in most general use. It may vary to the fraction of an inch in size, but never more. It is always a nice size; fits everybody's mouth, and gives universal satisfaction. A person who may turn away from the other kisses, is sure to appreciate this.

The quality of kisses cannot better be set forth than in the following quotations from the poets :—

THE COLD KISS.

"Cold is the kiss that *senseless* beauty gives."—*Sannazar.*

"Cold grew the lips, and cold,
Colder the kiss."—*Byron.*

"The very ice of chastity is in them."—*Shakespeare.*

"Those cold, cold kisses whence no rapture flows."
Secundus.

THE WARM KISS.

"O take this warm kiss on thy pale cold lips."
Shakespeare.

> "O Jannie, let me freely taste
> Those kisses warm and sweet,
> For which, my love, I'd gladly waste
> Whole ages at thy feet."

THE LONG KISS.

"A long, long kiss, a kiss of youth and love."—*Byron.*

> "A kiss
> Long as my exile, sweet as my revenge."—*Shakespeare.*

"The long kiss, when lips to lips adhere."—*Secundus.*

"And fix, in ecstacy of bliss,
On thy fair lips—one long—one never-ending kiss."
—*Secundus.*

> "One kiss the maiden gives, one last
> Long kiss."—*Moore.*

THE HUMID KISS.

"So, when thy humid lips encounter mine,
Sweet is the humid kiss which flows from thine."
—*Secundus.*

"The humid kiss with nectar rich imbued."—*Muret.*

> "Give me, sweet life, the kiss that's ripe,
> With honied moisture sweet."—*Bonnefons.*

> "And her moist lip to mine applied,
> And dewy kisses press'd."—*Bonnefons.*

The Sacred Kiss.

"Grow to my lips thou sacred kiss,
　On which my soul's beloved swore."—*Moore.*

"When from those lips, unbreathed upon for years,
I shall again kiss off the soul-felt tears,
And find those tears warm as when last they started,
Those sacred kisses pure as when we parted."—*Moore.*

"Now, by the jealous queen of heaven, that kiss
I carried from thee, dear, and my true lip
Hath virgin'd it e'er since."—*Shakespeare.*

The Soft Kiss.

"Our praises are our wages, you may ride us
With one soft kiss a thousand furlongs, ere
With spur we heat an acre."—*Shakespeare.*

"While my heart with passion glowing,
　Calls thee loveliest, dearest, best,
Wilt thou, the soft kiss bestowing,
　Soothe its pain, and give it rest."—*Bonnefons.*

The Ardent Kiss.

"So ardent kisses ardent joys impart,
And the warm transport thrills within the breast."
Secundus.

The Zealous Kiss.

"Upon thy cheek lay I this zealous kiss
As seal to the indenture of my love."—*Shakespeare.*

"Your lips, dear maid, the *thrilling* kiss impart."
Secundus.

"'Give me, sweet maid, one *little* kiss,
One little kiss,' I said, and sighed."—*Secundus*.

"And seal the title with a *lovely* kiss."—*Shakespeare*.

"While now her bending neck she plies
Backward to meet the *burning* kiss,
Then with an easy cruelty denies
Yet wishes you would snatch, not ask the prize."
Horace.

"*Mild* as the kisses of connubial love."—*Kirke White*.

"What lack we here to crown our bliss,
While thus the pulse of joy beats high?
What but fair woman's *yielding* kiss,
Her panting breath and melting eye."
Sir Walter Scott.

How to Kiss.

A PERSON who confessed to not knowing how to kiss would be looked upon as a natural curiosity, or a heathen of the worst type, and yet, even in this civilised land, there are lots of people who are quite ignorant of the art! They are in the habit of doing something with their lips, which they call kissing, but it is nothing of the sort—they deceive themselves! There are kisses, and there are KISSES, and the difference between them is as black is to white, or heat to cold. The art of kissing is very

easy and simple, although so many people bungle over it. Proficiency in it is attained by practice—practice makes perfect. Kissing requires to be done with great care and deliberation. Kisses that are made in a hurry are never perfect, they are deformed or fragmentary, and would not pass for anything in the Courts of Love. There are single and *double* kisses. The former are not bad in their way, but lack the very thing which the latter possesses—reciprocity. The double kiss can only be made by the united effort of two persons—a kiss must be given and received simultaneously by each.

The following instructions are given by Dr. Piesse, and are well worth the careful consideration of all persons interested in the subject:—

"People will kiss, yet not one in a hundred knows how to extract bliss from lovely lips, any more than he knows how to make diamonds from charcoal. And yet it is easy, at least for us. First know whom you are going to kiss. Don't make a mistake, although a mistake may be good. Don't jump like a trout for a fly, and smack a good woman on the neck, on the ear, on the corner of her forehead, or on the end of her nose. The gentleman should be a little the taller. He should have a clean face, a kind eye, and a mouth full of expression. Don't kiss everybody. Don't sit down to it; stand up. Need not be anxious about getting in a crowd. Two persons are plenty to corner, and catch a kiss; more persons would spoil the sport. Take the left hand of the lady in your right; let your hat go to—any place out of the way: place the left hand gently over the shoulder of the lady, and let it fall down the right side, towards the belt. Her head will fall lightly upon your shoulder—and a handsome shoulder strap it makes. Don't be in a hurry; send a little life down your left arm. Her left hand is in your right; let there be an impression to that, not like the grip of a vice, but a gentle clasp, full of electricity, thought, and respect. Don't be in a hurry. Her head lies carelessly on your shoulder. You are nearly heart to heart. Look down into her half-closed eyes. Gently, yet manfully, press her to your bosom. Stand firm. Be brave, but don't be in a hurry. Her lips are almost open. Lean slightly forward with your head, not the body. Take good aim; the lips meet; the eyes close; the heart opens; the soul rides the storms, troubles, and sorrows of life (don't be in a hurry); heaven opens before you; the world shoots under your feet as a meteor flashes across the evening sky (don't be afraid); the nerves dance before the just erected altar of love, as zephyrs dance with the dew-trimmed flowers; the heart forgets its bitterness, and the art of kissing is learned. No fuss, no noise, no fluttering. Kissing don't hurt; it don't require a gold band to make it legal."

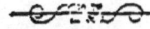

When to Kiss, and when Not.

IT is not everyone who knows exactly when to kiss, and when to abstain; it requires great discrimination, and, at times, no small amount of self-denial and resolution. It is impossible to lay down any particular rules for guidance in such a matter. Circumstances alter cases, and in kissing, a great deal depends on the circumstances. A few general rules may be observed with advantage:— Kiss as often as you can, within the bounds of propriety. Never let a favourable opportunity slip by;

if it is not very favourable, never mind, don't give way to grief. You need not trouble to ask a lady if you may kiss her, ladies are as fond of kisses as gentlemen, and probably more so. If you ask permission, remember that

> "Maids in modesty say *No*, to that
> Which they would have the profferer construe *Ay*."
> TWO GENT. OF VERONA, act i. sc. 2.

In courtship there are many proper occasions for kisses, don't overlook them. Always kiss on meeting and parting with your sweetheart, even if you omit doing so in the interval. Whenever you take a young lady out, take a kiss as well, if she should remonstrate with you (if she is a sensible girl she won't) have in readiness, and humbly tender her this Shakesperian apology:—

> "I were unmannerly to take you out
> And not to kiss you."—HENRY VIII., act i. sc. 4.

If that don't answer, be magnanimous, and return the kiss:—Part friendly—you will understand each other better next time.

Avoid kissing in a railway train. The dangers of that means of locomotion need no augmenting. If perchance your valour should overcome your discretion while passing through the tunnel, and you kiss the lady next to you, do it quietly and deliberately, otherwise you may make the other ladies jealous on hearing the salute, or, what would be worse, make the particular lady blush, and identify her with a transaction that might result unpleasantly. Kissing a stranger on the railway is always more or less dangerous. Try to avoid such a collision.

If you are in the connubial state you have ample opportunity for osculation in the bosom of your own family. It is not well to kiss a young widow too soon after her bereavement; better wait a week or two till she gets over it. When adverse circumstances compel, "kiss the rod" with all humility; it will do you no harm, indeed you might kiss it periodically with advantage to yourself and others.

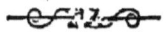

Kisses in Courtship.

"I can express no kinder sign of love
Than this kind kiss."—2 HENRY VI., act i. sc. 1.

COURTSHIP would be nothing without kisses, they are a *sine quâ non* at that interesting period of life. Kisses first break the ice, and bring the blushing lovers *face to face*, and kisses gently fan the fire of love. The wooer may, like Othello, be little able to "grace his cause" in speaking for himself,—he may tell but a faltering and stammering tale of love in his sweetheart's

"See how they kiss and court!"
TAMING OF THE SHREW, act iv. sc. 2.

ear,—he may make a mull of it, but his impassioned

kisses will speak for him to her lips and heart with no uncertain sound, and woo her with other eloquence than words. When the lady happens to be the wooer, kisses are just as potent. Here is proof—

> " O, the kindest Kate !—
> She hung about my neck, and kiss on kiss
> She vied so fast, protesting oath on oath,
> That in a twink she won me to her love."
> TAMING OF THE SHREW, act ii. sc. 1.

In courtship a kiss has frequently to supply the place of a word, and it is wonderful how much a few of them improve a sentence and make its meaning felt. Kisses

cannot be used too freely in courtship, that is, between the parties concerned, but zealous care must be taken that they do not extend further. A single kiss misplaced has often caused a catastrophe,—blown up the whole magazine of love! There are times when kisses, however chaste, are highly dangerous, especially to lovers and newly-married people. The Green-eyed monster will put in an appearance, and when he does it is no easy matter to get rid of him.

When true lovers meet, the kisses of courtship are the most rapturous that lips can produce or heart conceive! They are as full of bliss as an egg is of meat; especially those following the "popping" of the question, and its satisfactory answer. It is usual also to seal the affair with a "holy kiss."

When lovers no longer relish each others kisses more than their daily food, or aught beside, depend upon it "there is something rotten in the state of Denmark," and the sooner it is looked into the better. They will do well to pause before approaching the hymeneal altar, and, it may be, do better by making up their minds to "kiss and part."

The osculation of courtship does not last for ever. After a while (long while sometimes) the end draws near. The happy day at last arrives, the bridegroom meets his bride,

"And claims her with a loving kiss."

They are married, and it may be, done for! Their kisses then are connubial,—very good kisses and palatable for an indefinite period, after which there is a danger, yea, even a probability that they will deteriorate in quality and decrease in quantity!

The following convincing argument from Shakespeare's Comedy of "All's Well that Ends Well," shows the value of kisses in courtship—

"*Rosalind.*—Come, woo me; for now I am in a holiday humour, and like enough to consent. What would you say to me now, an I were your very, very Rosalind?

Orlando.—I would kiss you before I spoke.

Rosalind.—Nay, you were better speak first, and when you were gravelled for lack of matter, you might take occasion to kiss. Very good orators, when they are out, they will spit; and for lovers lacking (God warn us!) matter, the cleanliest shift is to kiss.

Orlando.—How if the kiss be denied?

Rosalind.—Then she puts you to entreaty, and there begins new matter."—Act iv. sc. 1.

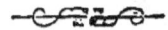

The Flavour & Fragrance of Kisses.

KISSES, of course, have no real flavour or fragrance about them. When they are spoken of as sweet, luscious, honied, perfumed, fragrant, &c., the language is but figurative, and means only that they are agreeable. Kissing is more a question of feeling than taste or smell. The bliss of kissing is caused by the union of the lips, and is more or less exquisite as the person kissed is more or less dear.—But stay! there's a mistake somewhere. Kisses at times have both taste and smell, and to the truth of that assertion here are three ugly witnesses—

Some of the fairer sex have rather a weakness for indulging in that strong vegetable known to us as the onion, although well knowing that for a certain time afterwards it spoils them for kissing. There are, of course, exceptions. Some young ladies would not eat an onion for the world, except on very extraordinary occasions. Noble-minded, self-denying creatures. They really deserve kissing! A strong-minded woman on reading this, may somewhat indignantly exclaim, "A pretty libel this on our sex! Don't the gentlemen eat onions too?—and besides, what about these malodorous things?"

We must here acknowledge our own weakness. The little luxuries portrayed above convict us. We had better drop the subject. Before doing so, however, let us hear what Shakespeare says:

"*Speed* (*reading aloud*).—Item. She is not to be kissed fasting in respect to her breath.

Lance.—Well, that may be mended by a breakfast. Read on.

Speed.—Item. She hath a sweet mouth.

Lance.—That makes amends for her sour breath."

Two Gent. Verona, act iii. sc. 1.

And here is something written by the great Dibdin—

"Celia hath sworn to love till death;
For words so full of bliss
I could have long'd, but for her breath,
To steal an ardent kiss."

Onions are fragrant indeed compared to sour breath. If the breath is not sweet, neither will the kisses be. A person with fœtid breath might even eat

"garlic
To mend the kissing with."
WINTER'S TALE, act iv. sc. 3.

If your sweetheart some day (or night) turns away when you are about to give the accustomed kiss, or, after receiving it, makes a wry face, begin to suspect yourself, and, if you discover that your breath is the cause, use every means of cure, or, depend upon it, you will lose what Celia lost, and probably a great deal more.

A fictitious flavour and fragrance may be given to kisses by the use of sweetmeats, but the practice is objectionable. Sugared kisses are apt to be sticky! Kisses are never better than when pure and simple.

(*Monkey.*) "If I were a woman I would kiss as many of you as had beards that pleased me, complexions that liked me, and breaths that I defied not; and, I am sure, as many as have good beards, or good faces, or sweet

breaths, will, for my kind offer, when I make curt'sy, bid me farewell."   As You Like It. [Epilogue.]

Kissing by Deputy.

It is very injudicious to send kisses through a third person. A complimentary message, or even one of love, may be conveyed by a friend—but kisses never! Always do your own kissing, and then you will have the satisfaction of knowing that it is *properly* done. Remember the old saying—"If you want a thing *done*, send your man to do it; but if you want it *well done*, do it yourself."

there is no zephyr they will go all the same without. Kisses thus forwarded, naturally lose much of their fragrance on the "desert air." They are never so good as when delivered from mouth to mouth, but, as there are times when lips cannot come near each other, it is convenient and pleasant to have a means of transport for kisses. You may chance to see your adored in a crowd, and not be able to get near her,—you may catch sight of her in a passing train, or, it may be, "up in a balloon"— she may put her head out of the window above when you are serenading her,—under all these circumstances, and many others, it is very nice to be able to waft her a kiss or more, and receive others in return. It may be here noted that kisses thus conveyed occasionally miscarry. To prevent that keep your eye fixed on the lady and take good aim. If you turn your eye, even for a moment, the kiss may alight on someone else and cause mischief.

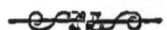

Kisses per Post.

KISSES are often transmitted through the post, sealed up in an ordinary envelope, and not even registered to indicate the value—they are also sent on halfpenny post cards— the latter method, however, is to be deprecated. Kisses are sacred, and should not be exposed to the vulgar gaze of letter sorters and postmen—besides they might steal them! Give them opportunities of stealing postage stamps from your letters if you like, but do not tempt them with valuable kisses! Consider the frailty of human nature. The following is a very common way of sending kisses, and the best also, because they are made *visible,*—thus :—

* * * * * * * * * * *

* * * * * * * * * *

It is nonsense to *say* you have sent lots of kisses, or a thousand, or ten thousand, for, if none are visible the recipient has only your bare word for it. Kisses are sometimes sent on a flower or leaf, or enclosed in a locket, &c. All very neat ways of sending, but the kisses are apt to be overlooked and lost, as the *material* object first attracts the eye and, it may be, the heart.

Cost of Kisses.

KISSES are very easily made. It is no trouble at all to make them—on the other hand a pleasure. Anyone with a pair of lips—all the tools required—can produce them in any quantity—thousands per day, if need be, and yet, kisses sometimes come expensive, varying in price from a few pounds to as many hundreds! A kiss often costs a box on the ears by the young lady, or perhaps a kick or two from her papa, but if the kiss is anything like a good one it can scarcely be thought dear at the price. Sometimes a kiss costs a world of sighs,—a heap of trouble, many artful dodges, wiles and stratagems, but even then it may be cheap. If a man is desirous of purchasing a costly kiss, he may easily gratify his desire —let him take a walk in some fashionable street or promenade, and when he meets a stern-looking old gentleman with a charming young lady by his side, and a smart young fellow who appears to be "sweet" on the latter, he must rush to the charmer, clasp her lovingly to his bosom, kiss her lips fervently, and when the two gentlemen ask him what he means, knock them both down! If the kiss does not cost him dear, kisses will never be *dear* again. There are many other ways of obtaining costly kisses, but it is not worth while to

Kisses per Post.

KISSES are often transmitted through the post, sealed up in an ordinary envelope, and not even registered to indicate the value—they are also sent on halfpenny post cards—the latter method, however, is to be deprecated. Kisses are sacred, and should not be exposed to the vulgar gaze of letter sorters and postmen—besides they might steal them! Give them opportunities of stealing postage stamps from your letters if you like, but do not tempt them with valuable kisses! Consider the frailty of human nature. The following is a very common way of sending kisses, and the best also, because they are made *visible*,—thus:—

* * * * * * * * * * *

* * * * * * * * * *

It is nonsense to *say* you have sent lots of kisses, or a thousand, or ten thousand, for, if none are visible the recipient has only your bare word for it. Kisses are sometimes sent on a flower or leaf, or enclosed in a locket, &c. All very neat ways of sending, but the kisses are apt to be overlooked and lost, as the *material* object first attracts the eye and, it may be, the heart.

Cost of Kisses.

KISSES are very easily made. It is no trouble at all to make them—on the other hand a pleasure. Anyone with a pair of lips—all the tools required—can produce them in any quantity—thousands per day, if need be, and yet, kisses sometimes come expensive, varying in price from a few pounds to as many hundreds! A kiss often costs a box on the ears by the young lady, or perhaps a kick or two from her papa, but if the kiss is anything like a good one it can scarcely be thought dear at the price. Sometimes a kiss costs a world of sighs,—a heap of trouble, many artful dodges, wiles and stratagems, but even then it may be cheap. If a man is desirous of purchasing a costly kiss, he may easily gratify his desire—let him take a walk in some fashionable street or promenade, and when he meets a stern-looking old gentleman with a charming young lady by his side, and a smart young fellow who appears to be "sweet" on the latter, he must rush to the charmer, clasp her lovingly to his bosom, kiss her lips fervently, and when the two gentlemen ask him what he means, knock them both down! If the kiss does not cost him dear, kisses will never be *dear* again. There are many other ways of obtaining costly kisses, but it is not worth while to specify them—such kisses never give satisfaction—they are worthless! Kisses that are dear to the *heart* are infinitely better than those that are dear only to the *pocket*. It it a familiar saying that "Stolen kisses are sweet," but it all depends upon whom they are stolen from. Kisses may happen to be anything but sweet.

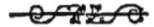

The healing Virtue of Kisses.

THE healing virtue of kisses is very extraordinary. Kisses are very curative. They effected wonderful cures on many of us in our infantile days. Whenever (and it was often) we "came to grief," or grief came to us, by reason of an unlucky fall, violent contact with an article of furniture, or other mishap, the maternal kiss, judiciously applied to the injured part, never failed to give relief, and repeated applications to effect a perfect cure!

Kisses not only cure infantile hurts, but are very efficacious in many ailments of the adult. When a man is *sick* at heart; when his spirit is *wounded*, or when his feelings are *hurt*, what medicine will do him so much good as the sweet kisses administered to him freely by the loved ones? What will cure him of his ill-temper, and stop the angry words even on the threshold of his mouth better than a kiss? If a lady has a fit of sighing, what will cure her so easily and pleasantly as a kiss? A kiss has been known to give relief in face-ache, tooth-ache, heart-ache, and nearly every other ache or pain that flesh is heir to. And then, what a wonderful salve for the lips; kisses will keep them soft and pliable, and prevent their cracking. Kisses are wonderful in their medicinal action —they are either soothing or stimulating,—heating or cooling as may be desired, and always very tonic. The medicine is very agreeable to take—inexpensive—and

"Who was it caught me when I fell,
And kissed the place to make it well?
My Mother."

efficacious—one of natures simplest remedies. If we took it oftener, recommended it to our neighbours—and gave it to our neediest friends—there is no knowing what good results might follow.

Kiss in the Ring.

KISS in the Ring is a capital out-door game, much in vogue with the young people on such occasions as pic-nics, Sunday-school treats, or other pleasure parties where there is a good sprinkling of both sexes. The game is also popular with grown-up people, and there is no

reason why it should not be. There are few prettier sights to be seen at a pleasure-party than a good game of Kiss in the Ring, and few enjoyments more agreeable to the players. As long as kissing is so sweet, the game will ever be popular, despite all that has been said against it by those whom it is almost flattery to call Christians. *Honi soit qui mal y pense.*

For the information of those who may be ignorant of the game, we may briefly say that it is played thus:— A number (say a dozen) of boys, and about the same number of girls (to establish a sort of equilibrium of the sexes) form a large circle by joining hands. One player remains out of the ring, and, if a boy, commences the game by walking or running round the outside of the ring and tapping the back of any girl of his fancy; he then passes on as though nothing had happened; the girl upon receiving the gentle intimation, immediately leaves her place and runs in an opposite direction to that taken by him, when, lo! such is the magic of a circle, they both meet somewhere on the opposite side. After embracing and mutually exchanging kisses, they separate, and whichever reaches the vacant place first, falls in, and leaves the other out in the cold! The one thus left remains out until he or she is able to displace someone else in a similar manner. There is a great deal of cheating, or rather unfairness, in this game, sometimes, as there is in most others. We have known boys *manage* to keep out of a place in the ring till they had kissed all the pretty girls in succession! Girls have also been detected in a like wickedness! Such delinquency merits severe punishment. Perhaps the case might be met by compelling the delinquent to submit to a given number of kisses from the ugliest member of the opposite sex who happened to be playing in the game.

Forbidden Fruit.

IT does not do to kiss everybody—the line must be drawn somewhere. There is the "forbidden fruit" that may not be touched. The temptation to kiss a pretty girl, though a stranger, at first sight, may be very strong, but it must be overcome. As a rule, kisses should follow on a better acquaintance. Persons who kiss should at least know each other, unless they kiss under privileged circumstances. Some of the forbidden fruit is perfectly

"There is not half a kiss to choose."
WINTER'S TALE, act iv. sc. 3.

safe—no one would attempt to steal it, though the possessors may be frail!

A married man, and father of a family, should refrain from kissing his pretty maid-servants. It is never beneficial. Ten to one if it pleases his wife. It is very nice to have an agreeable neighbour—so handy to pop in for a chat with him, and there is no harm in loving your neighbour as yourself, but if he has a wife you must not entertain the same love for her. Keep at a respectful distance—never attempt to kiss her—it is forbidden fruit. Take heed to what Horace says:—

> "Never, ah, never kiss your neighbour's wife,
> For see what thousand mischiefs round you rise,
> And few the pleasures, tho' you gain the prize."

It is awkward and unpleasant to make such a blunder as to kiss the wrong person, and yet blunders of that kind are sometimes made—generally when a snatch has been made for the forbidden fruit! Always be *sure* of your intended victim before perpetrating the deed, and never snatch a kiss if it can be avoided—there is great danger that you may snatch it from the tip of her nose or chin, or any other part of the face except the lips.

Miscellaneous Kisses.

KISSING is not confined to mankind alone. Nature is so full of kisses that they may be seen and heard on every hand. The birds of the air kiss, and do it nicely too. Animals lick and fondle each other, and kiss in their own peculiar way, and even fishes are acquainted with the art

"And kiss like native things."
ALL'S WELL THAT ENDS WELL, act i. sc. 1.

Birds and animals and fishes not only kiss their own species, but are even condescending enough to kiss human beings! If a beautiful woman condescends to kiss a cat or dog it may, perhaps, not be considered *infra dig.* on the animal's part to kiss her in return! Some extraordinary kisses may sometimes be observed at the Zoological Gardens,—the most curious of which are those of the sea-lion, who at the call of a man, comes out of the water to bestow them upon him. Sea-lions will not kiss everybody; kissing with them, as with us, "goes by favour." The leaves on the trees kiss each other. The bee kisses the flower. The mountains kiss the heavens. The moonbeams kiss the sea; beside which the poets tell us of hundreds of kisses.—Kisses are here, there, and everywhere,—we even find

Kisses in the Oven!

The oven is the last place where one would think of looking for kisses, and yet they may often be found there! The loaves of bread as they lie baking in their tins, side by side, sometimes have a disposition to kiss. They get closer and closer to each other till at last their lips meet, and they kiss! So strong is the attachment springing up

between them, that they will not separate till forced to do so! Where the loaves have kissed, the crust is called "kissing crust," and hence it is the sweetest and nicest part of the loaf. In cakes the plums and currants frequently get close together, and kiss each other. The more kisses that are possible in a cake, the better it is, and more worthy of the name of "Kissing Cake."

Kisses in the Cup.

Kisses often find their way into the cup, it matters not whether it contains wine, tea, coffee, or what not. They float about on the surface of the liquid and may either be taken off with the lips or with a spoon. But, after all, they are not worth much,—frothy and

insipid. Such kisses may serve the turn of persons (and there are such) who have little chance of getting better ones, but they are not esteemed by those who have access to pretty lips.

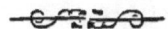

An Easy Way of Making Gloves.

LADY has the advantage over a gentleman in respect to gloves. She may often win a pair, or half-a-dozen pairs, or more, by betting with a gentleman on the result of a boat or horse race. Of course, if she loses, he will not expect her to pay (as a rule she won't) and oftentimes, if he is spooney, he will make her a present of the gloves to console her for losing! And then, again, a lady has an opportunity of acquiring a pair of gloves cheap by keeping her eyes open.

If, after a day's fatigue, or from some other cause, a gentleman should happen to fall asleep in the presence of a lady, she has but to kiss him, and that entitles her to a pair of kid gloves at the sleeper's cost. This may be described on his part as *kid-napping*, and on hers as *kid-nabbing*. Gentlemen! beware of drowsiness when you are in the company of ladies you don't like. If you like your company, and don't mind the cost of a few pairs of gloves, it won't matter if you do go to sleep a time or two in the course of an evening, but never allow yourself to be caught shamming!

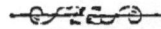

Whist—Kissing the Dealer.

OF all indoor amusements for a select party, the game of Whist is perhaps the most popular. A couple of gentlemen, and as many ladies may play at it a long time without getting fatigued. Ladies are an acquisition to the game (unless the players are old and crusty), and though they may sometimes, through carelessness, lose the "odd trick" or spoil their partner's "little game," their participation in the amusement is desirable, if not

profitable; beside, is there not the chance of a kiss? True it may be somewhat remote, but never mind, you must wait, and if no earlier opportunity occurs, there is a chance that this may.—When four cards have been thrown out, one by each player, the numbers on which run consecutively, thus, 1, 2, 3, 4, the person playing the fourth card may claim to kiss the dealer. If the dealer happens to be of your own sex you need not trouble to take the kiss you are entitled to, but, if of the opposite sex, you may as well stand on your rights, as the ladies now make such a vigorous stand on theirs.

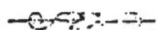

Kissing the Hand or Foot.

IT was a Greek custom for an inferior person to kiss the hand of a superior, as a token of respect and humility, and when the superiority was so great as between a sovereign and a vassal, the latter was privileged to fall prostrate and kiss the foot of the former! There is not much foot-kissing done in the present day. Sovereigns, as a rule are less exacting, and even thankful to have their hands kissed, if it be done sincerely. The infallible

"Then kiss his foot."—TITUS ANDRONICUS, act i. sc. 3.

old man who holds sway at the Vatican still exposes his holy foot for the labial salute, and occasionally receives it. We have nothing to say against *him*.

There can be little objection to kissing a person's hand—if it be clean, and the custom fashionable, but to kiss the foot is a very different matter. The foot is so very *low*. Byron, in preferring the hand to the foot, says—

> "Here is an honourable compromise,
> A half-way house of diplomatic rest."

The Bard of Avon makes frequent allusion to kissing of the hand, especially as appertaining to royalty.—Thus:—

> "Lord Marshal, let me kiss my sovereign's hand
> And bow my knee before his majesty."
> RICH. III., act i. sc. 1.

> "In sign of truth I kiss your highness' hand."
> 2 HENRY VI., act iv. sc. 8.

> "Behold this man;
> Commend unto his lips thy favouring hand;—
> Kiss it, my warrior."
> ANT. & CLEO., act iv. sc. 8.

> "I will kiss thy royal fingers, and take leave."
> LOVE'S LABOUR LOST, act v. sc. 2.

> "O could this kiss be printed in thy hand,
> That thou might'st think upon these, by the seal
> Through whom a thousand sighs are breath'd for thee."
> 2 HENRY VI., act iii. sc. 2.

> "There is gold, and here
> My bluest veins to kiss; a hand that kings
> Have lipp'd, and trembled kissing."
> ANT. & CLEO., act ii. sc. 5.

"I kiss these fingers for eternal peace."

1 HENRY VI., act v. sc. 3.

The custom is still more or less observed in polite society. A gentleman is ever ready to acknowledge a lady's superiority by kissing her hand, although he may be very reluctant to do the same by one of his own sex. Kissing a lady's hand is not to be compared to kissing her lips, but still it is a privilege not to be despised when the greater one cannot be enjoyed. The hand is a convenient stepping-stone to the lips, as the artful lover well knows. If a lady wishes to keep her lips to herself, she must not allow gentlemen to kiss her hand too freely. Ladies may court kisses through the medium of their hands. The fact did not escape the notice of Sir Walter Raleigh, for he thus wrote:—

> "Were her hands as rich a prize
> As her hair, or precious eyes,
> If she laid them out to take
> Kisses, for good manners' sake;
> And let ev'ry lover skip
> From her hand unto her lip;
> If she seem not chaste to me,
> What care I how chaste she be?"

"Why, this is he
That kiss'd away his hand in courtesy."

LOVE'S LABOUR LOST, act v. sc. 2.

Lips.

LIPS are essential to kissing, and the kisses vary in bliss as the lips are more or less convenient for the purpose. The best kind of lips are those that are a little prominent and full. Pouting lips are not the worst kind. Some people are not blessed with lips, they have but the bare *edges* of the mouth. When the mouth is shut the edges fit closely together, and form a perfectly flat surface from the nose to the chin. To kiss such is like kissing a table or door, and quite as blissful. The kisses are as

"Mark you his lips."
CORIOLANUS, act. i. sc. 2.

flat as pancakes. Some lips are soft as velvet, and others as hard as flint—some are warm and exquisite to the touch, and others are as "dead as a door nail." The lips are very susceptible to emotions. They blanch with fear and burn with love—quiver with rage, curl with scorn, &c.—

> "O what a deal of scorn looks beautiful
> In the contempt and anger of his lip!"
> TWELFTH NIGHT, act iii. sc. 1.

> "Teach not thy lip such scorn; for it was made
> For kissing, lady, not for such contempt."
> RICHARD III., act i. sc. 2.

To a careless observer all lips are about the same colour, but such is not the case, they are of various hues. It is a matter of opinion which is the best. Persons who are fond of kissing are "not to a shade," and, on seeing a pretty girl, are ever ready to say with Byron:—

> "Whene'er I view those lips of thine
> Their hue invites my fervent kiss."

The different hues are mentioned in the following quotations:—

> "I saw her *coral* lips to move
> And with her breath she did perfume the air."
> TAMING OF THE SHREW, act i. sc. 1.

> "That I might touch!
> But kiss; one kiss!—*Rubies* unparagon'd."
> CYMBELINE, act ii. sc. 2.

"Around those lips with *crimson* dyed."—*Secundus*.

"There's a sweet and winning cunning
 In her bright lip's *crimson* hue,
And a flitting tint of roses
 From her soft cheek gleaming through."
F. A. Fuller.

"In those lips of *rosy* hue
 Pain and pleasure mingled lie,
Oh! how sweetly they undo,
 By how many arts destroy."—*Bonnefons.*

"Sweet are those lips so *ruby* bright."—*Bonnefons.*

"Those *ruby* lips where balmy nectar flows."—*Secundus.*

"A hundred sweet kisses, by hundreds told o'er,
I'll give those *red* lips, my dear charmer, of thine."
Secundus.

"Touch but my lips with those fair lips of thine
 (Though mine be not so fair, yet are they *red*),
The kiss shall be thine own as well as mine."—*Lucrece.*

"Two lips indifferent red."
TWELFTH NIGHT, act i. sc. 5.

"When lovers' lips in transport join
 Their souls to share that transport fly,
And, as their mingling breaths combine,
 The *purple* gems with life supply."—*Guarini.*

"Let thy lips that breathe perfume
 Deeper *purple* now assume."

"Their lips were four red roses on a stalk
Which, in their summer beauty, kiss'd each other."
                                RICHARD III., act iv. sc. 3.

"A cherry lip."
                                RICHARD III., act i. sc. 1

"That womankind had but one rosy mouth,
To kiss them all at once, from north to south."
                                Byron.

"Divers philosophers hold that the lips is parcel of the mouth." MERRY WIVES OF WINDSOR, act i. sc. 1.

"Once more the ruby-coloured portal open'd,
Which to his speech did honey passage yield."
                                VENUS AND ADONIS.

Under the Mistletoe.

ONCE every year a glorious time comes round for people who are fond of kissing. When the Holly, with it ruby berries greets the eye, and its fair sister, the Mistletoe, with its pearly berries gladdens the heart,—at the season, above all others, sacred to feasting and merry-

making, the Festival of Kisses is held. The mystic

Mistletoe then grants to all, whether old or young, special license to kiss. In the mansions of the rich, as well as in the humble dwellings of the poor, the Mistletoe bough finds a place; the girls take care of that. It is female hands alone that generally " hang the mistletoe high in the hall "—ay, and in the kitchen too—in all sorts of sly corners and secret places, and woe, or rather anything but woe, betide the person who unwarily strolls beneath it—somebody is sure to creep up behind, or suddenly spring from some unlikely quarter, to administer a surprising kiss. When the Mistletoe appears, jealousy has to be put on one side or swallowed. Sweethearts may kiss anybody else, married people may do the same; in fact, anybody may kiss anybody else, and everybody everybody else! Married people enjoy the freedom quite as much as single, and some of the old quite as much as the young. The happy time only occurring annually (some would have it continually), it is naturally looked forward to with longing eagerness by certain persons, as it gives them the opportunity of parting with kisses, that, owing to their natural modesty, they may have had on their lips for months. If a girl is too bashful to lead an unsuspecting gentleman under the Mistletoe, and then inflict on him the sweet penalty, she may take frequent occasion to pass under it herself, and if there are any gentlemen about she will not have to wait long for a kiss. In the innocence (or artfulness) of her nature, she may then blushingly say—

" 'Twas not my purpose thus to beg a kiss;
I am ashamed; O heavens, what have I done?"
TROILUS AND CRESSIDA, act iii. sc. 2.

The Mistletoe feast is of indefinite length: it may last a week or fortnight, or it may extend over months, it all depends upon the disposition of the persons interested. Mistletoe is sometimes kept about till it has completely dried up. That is using it rather hard! Kissing that could be done under dried-up Mistletoe could be as well done without it. There is a time for all things, and so there is a time for the girls to take down the Mistletoe bough; we leave it to their discretion.

Kisses in Song.

KISSING is by far too sweet a subject to have been overlooked by song-writers. Kisses in song have found their way to every mouth (or ought to have done). What is more enchanting than to hear a mortal nymph singing "Kiss me Quick and Go," or "Kiss me and Call me your Own," unless it is to answer the appeal? Kiss songs are very numerous, and very popular, especially with the fairer sex. A young lady may be ever so shy and modest, but is sure to be familiar with a few oscula-

tory songs. "Let me Kiss him for his Mother,"—"Kiss but Never Tell," and "Stolen Kisses are the Sweetest," are great favourites with both sexes. The kisses which have left a fair singer's lips in *song*, not unfrequently find their way back again in reality.

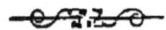

Kisses at Marriages.

IT is an old English custom for the bridegroom to kiss his wife at the conclusion of the marriage ceremony. Shakespeare makes the following allusion to it in the "Taming of the Shrew," act iii. sc. 2 :—

"He took the bride about the neck,
And kiss'd her lips with such a clamorous smack,
That, at the parting, all the church did echo!"

The custom is seldom observed now except among the lower classes. In the upper circles the bridegroom leaves the kissing part of the ceremony to be performed by the elderly relations of the bride. It may be noted that the Queen, at her marriage, was kissed by the Duke of Sussex, but not by Prince Albert.

Russian and German Customs.

THERE is a custom more or less observed in Russia, once a year, at Eastertide. After fasting the whole forty days of Lent, which the Russian professes to do, he naturally hails with no small amount of pleasure the day succeeding that abstemious period, and "goes in" for a few *natives*. He gets up early in the morning, and putting a coloured egg in his pocket and a pleasing smile on his face, sallies forth. He offers the egg to the first person he meets, who accepts it, and gives him another in return, and then the two exchange kisses! On this day the Russian is privileged to stop *anyone*, and offer him or her the exchange of an egg with the festal greeting; and so a young good-looking fellow has a good day's work before him. It is a remarkable fact (and yet, why should it be?) that two persons of the same sex rarely happen to meet on such a day!

It is the custom in Germany for a man who is engaged to a girl to salute, upon making his adieu for the evening, the whole of the family, beginning with the mother. Thus, in a family circle embracing half-a-dozen girls, each having a lover, no less than forty-eight kisses would have to be given on the occasion of a united meeting; and when we consider that each lover would give his own sweetheart ten times as many kisses as he gave her sisters, the grand total would outnumber a hundred!

Kisses and Colds.

A KISS and a cold should never meet, they are incompatible. The latter completely destroys the former. A kiss is blissful when its nectar comes from the gods; but anything but that if the nectar comes from *above*. The difference is that one is *Ambrosial* and the other *Nosial*. To be plain, when the nose runs, the would-be-kisser should run also. It is no time for a labial salute,—a pocket-handkerchief answers the purpose much better.

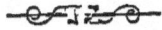

Kisses and Gapes.

IT is next to impossible to kiss the lips of anyone who is gaping, and if it be accomplished the pleasure must naturally be infinitesimal. Beside, there is danger in such an attempt. The following lines by an old writer are *apropos* :—

"Be thy mouth like jaws of death
That they who kiss must kiss thy teeth;

And hold by th' handle of thy chin
Lest their foot slip, and they fall in!
Yet, if thou wilt not gape on me
What care I how broad it be?"

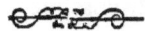

Omnium Gatherum.

THE instant I'm born, though my frame is quite weak,
Most wondrous to utter, I smartly can speak;
My parents are pleased, and greatly rejoice,
And seem quite enraptured to hear my sweet [voice;
But short, ah! too short is the time that I stay,
For when I've done speaking I languish away;
Yet this to my parents but seldom gives pain,
For they with a touch can call life back again!
Now, ye fair girls, and ye cheerful young swains,
Come search for my name and take me for your pains.
—A Kiss.

Why is a kiss like a rumour?—Because it goes from mouth to mouth.

When is a man like a spoon?—When he touches a lady's lips without kissing them.

Those who have tried it say that kissing is like a sewing-machine, because it *seams* nice.

If the Queen kissed the Prince of Wales, and he returned the compliment, what public building would it name?—The Royal Exchange.

It does not matter how watchful and vigilant a girl is, if a rude fellow kisses her, it is ten to one he will do it right under her nose!

What shape is a kiss?—A-lip-tickle!

Why are two young ladies kissing each other an emblem of Christianity?—Because they are doing to each other as they would men should do unto them.

Mock Turtles.—Kissing before company, and fighting afterwards.

What part of speech is a kiss?—A conjunction.

What flowers are there between a lady's nose and chin?—Tulips.

Why is a kiss like a sermon?—Because it requires, at least, two heads and an application.

When are kisses sweetest?—When *syrup*-titiously obtained.

If you were kissing a young lady who was very spooney, what would be her opinion of newspapers during the operation?—She would not want any "Spectators," nor "Observers," but lots of "Times."

What is the difference between an accepted and a rejected lover?—One kisses his misses; the other misses his kisses.

"My brother is shy—I am not shy at all,
So, when there's a mistletoe hung in our hall,
He manages always to miss all the kisses,
While *I*, on the contrary, kiss all the misses!"

We look out for a pretty *face* when we see the mistle-*toe*.

BREAD AND CHEESE AND KISSES.

" I would often ask her, being of an inquisitive turn of mind—' Mother, what have you got for dinner to-day?' 'Bread and Cheese and Kisses,' she would reply merrily. Then I knew that one of our favourite dishes was sure to be on the table, and I rejoiced accordingly. And to this day, Bread and Cheese and Kisses bears for me in its simple utterance a sacred and beautiful meaning. It means contentment: it means cheerfulness: it means the exercise of sweet words and gentle thought; it means Home!"

TWELVE HUNDRED KISSES!

The *Opinione* relates a curious peace-making ceremony which took place recently at Sedini. Twenty-nine families of eight districts of Anglona took a share in this solemn pact of peace. The bishop of the diocese, accompanied by five priests and by the authorities of the country, assisted at the ceremony. It began by the assembling in a large field near Sedini of the different groups of the parties interested, who afterwards formed into separate rows of offenders and offended by the assassinations committed or wounds inflicted by vendetta within the last ten years. Then, placing themselves opposite the bishop and prefect, they embraced each other two by two, at first with a certain reluctance, but by degrees the ice melted, and soon the greatest cordiality was manifested on both sides. The twenty-nine families, with their relations to the fourth generation, amounted in all to twelve hundred people, who thus exchanged the kiss of peace. A crowd of more than two thousand persons formed a circle round this interesting scene, which left a deep and most pleasing impression in all hearts. During the remainder of the day and on the following morning the most sincere joy and satisfaction were manifested on all sides, and will, it is hoped, be as lasting as it was solemnly celebrated.

Buss—to kiss. Re-bus—to kiss again. Blunder-bus—to kiss the wrong girl. Omni-bus—to kiss all the girls in the room. Bus-ter—a general kisser. *E pluri*-bus *unum*—a thousand kisses in one.

A MISSOURIAN who stole a kiss from a pretty girl, was fined by a magistrate, horsewhipped by her brother, and worried into a brain-fever by his wife. The clergyman also alluded to the affair in his sermon, the local editor took sides with the clergyman, and reviewed the case in print, and the potato-bug ate up every blade of the malefactor's crop!

STATIONERY.—" What ? " exclaimed the accomplished fashionable Fitzwiggle to the exquisitely lovely Miss De La Sparrowgrass, "what would you be, dearest, if I should press the stamp of love upon those sealing-wax lips?" " I," responded the fairy-like creature, "should be *Stationery!*"

SLIGHTLY ARTFUL.—An engaged young gentleman got rather neatly out of a scrape with his intended. She taxed him with having kissed two young ladies at some party at which she was not present. He owned it, but said that their united ages only made twenty-one. The simple-minded girl thought of ten and eleven, and laughed off her pout. He did not explain that one was nineteen and the other two years of age! Wasn't it artful? Just like the men!

A NEW YORK Judge has decided that kissing constitutes an engagement to marry, and that the marriageable person having been kissed by a marriageable person, can thereupon compel the kisser to marry the kissee, or else pay damages for breach of promise.

YOUNG men who go to see girls have adopted a new way of obtaining kisses. They assert, on the authority of scientific writers, that the concussion produced by a kiss will cause the flame of a gas-jet to flicker, and easily induce the girl to experiment in the interest of science.

The first kiss or two the parties watch the flame to see it flicker, but soon become so interested in the experiments as to let it flicker if it wants to. Try it yourself.

A LADY caught her husband kissing the servant girl. The doctor was sent for. He says he can patch up the face of her better-half, but he'll always be bald-headed!

A MAN in Jersey who had ravished a kiss from a school-girl, was fined by the magistrates, horsewhipped by her big brother, and scratched bald-headed by his own wife. And it was not much of a kiss after all!

THE youth who stole a kiss has been discharged on condition that he will not embrace another opportunity.

LOVERS AND THE MOON.—It was once the custom of Highland women to salute the new moon with a solemn courtesy. English country dames were wont to sit astride a stile or gate, waiting the new moon's appearance, to welcome her with, "A fine moon, God bless her!" Bachelors were privileged to claim a kiss and a pair of gloves upon announcing the advent of a new moon to the first maiden they met.

PLACARDS on the St. Louis street cars declare that "This car can't wait for ladies to kiss good-bye!"

An Iowa justice of the peace refused to fine a man for kissing a girl against her will, because, when the lass came into the court, he was obliged to hold on by the arms of his chair to keep from kissing her himself.

AMATEUR SURGERY.—A gentleman in Kentucky, under the influence of wine, undertook to kiss two young ladies at their house, but they retreated to their room; he followed. He got his leg through the door, but they fastened it there by pressure against the door, and, procuring a saw, amputated the leg below the knee. [The leg was a wooden one.]

KISSING HER BACK!—Little boy to his mamma: "Mamma, I have something to tell you—schoolmistress kissed me!" "Well, did you kiss her back?" "No, I kissed her *face*."

SOME time since a party of ladies and gentlemen went on a tour of inspection through Durham Castle. The "lions" were shown to them by an elderly female, of a sour, solemn, and dignified aspect. In the course of their peregrinations they came to the celebrated tapestry for which the castle is famed. "These," said the guide, in a true showman style, flavoured with a dash of piety to suit the subject, and pointing to several groups of figures upon the tapestry—"these represent scenes in the life of Jacob." "Oh, yes—how pretty!" said a young lady; and, with a laugh, pointing to two figures in somewhat close proximity, she continued, "I suppose that is Jacob kissing Rachel?" "No, madam," responded the indignant guide, with crushing dignity, "that is *Jacob wrestling with the angel.*" The men haw-hawed, the young lady subsided, and offered no further expository remarks, but groaned under a sense of unworthiness during the rest of the visit.

"KISSING your sweetheart," says a trifling young man, "is like eating soup with a fork; it takes a long time to get enough."

To prevent your hair coming off—never let your wife catch you kissing the servant girl."

A PRETTY Southend girl is a "mind reader." She said to her bashful beau the other evening, "La! I believe you are going to kiss me!" She was right.

A YOUNG lady being once asked whether the kiss, being a substantive, was proper or common, archly replied that it was *both* proper and common.

WHAT IS A REBUS?

"WHAT is a rebus?" I asked of dear Mary,
    As close to my side the dear maiden was seated;
I saw her eye sink and her countenance vary
    As she said in reply, " 'T is a kiss, sir, repeated."

"What is a rebus?" innocently asked a lovely miss of a black-eyed lad. Imprinting a kiss on her breathing lips, he replied, "If you now will return the compliment, that will be a re-bus." She was satisfied with the information.

"Ma, that nice young man, Mr. Sauftong, is very fond of kissing." "Mind your seam, Julia; who told you such nonsense?" "Ma, dear, I had it from his own lips."

"I saw Esau kissing Kate,
And the fact is we all three saw;
For I saw Esau, he saw me,
And she saw I saw Esau."

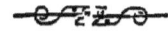

PART II.

Kisses in Poetry.

Shakespeare.

" I CAN express no kinder sign of love, than this kind kiss."

2 HENRY VI., act i. sc. 1.

"Come, kiss, and let us part."
TROILUS AND CRESSIDA, act iv. sc. 5.

"Injurious time, now, with a robber's haste,
Crams his rich thievery up, he know not how;
As many farewells as be stars in heaven,
With distinct breath and consigned kisses to them,

He fumbles up into a loose adieu;
And scants us with a single famish'd kiss,
Distasted with the salt of broken tears."

"O, the kindest Kate!—
She hung about my neck; and kiss on kiss
She vied so fast, protesting oath on oath,
That in a twink she won me to her love."
              TAMING OF THE SHREW, act ii. sc. I.

"*Katharina.*—Husband, let's follow, to see the end of
Pet.—First kiss me, Kate, and we will.   [this ado.

Kath.—What, in the midst of the street?
Pet.—What, art thou ashamed of me?
Kath.—No, sir; God forbid:—but ashamed to kiss.
Pet.—Why, then let's home again:—come, sirrah, let's away. [stay.
Kath.—Nay, I will give thee a kiss: now pray thee love,
Pet.—Is not this well? Come, my sweet Kate; better once than never, for never too late."

TAMING OF THE SHREW, act v. sc. 1.

"What were thy lips the worse for one poor kiss?"

" Thou shalt be worshipp'd, kiss'd, lov'd, and ador'd."
TWO GENTLEMEN OF VERONA, act iv. sc. 4.

"Let me unkiss the oath 'twixt thee and me;
And yet, not so, for with a kiss 'twas made."
                    RICHARD II., act v. sc. 1.

"I am dying, Egypt, dying; only
I here importune death a while, until
Of many thousand kisses the poor last
I lay upon thy lips."
              ANTONY AND CLEOPATRA, act iv. sc. 13.

"But if thou fall, O then imagine this,
    The earth, in love with thee, thy footing trips
And all is but to rob thee of a kiss.
    Rich preys make true men thieves; so do thy lips
Make modest Dian cloudy and forlorn,
    Lest she should steal a kiss, and die forsworn."

"Now let me say good night, and so say you;
    If you will say so you shall have a kiss.
'Good night,' quoth she; and ere he says adieu,
    The honey fee of parting tender'd is:

Her arms do lend his neck a sweet embrace,
Incorporate then they seem, face grows to face."

"*Agamemnon.*—Is this the Lady Cressid?
Diomed.— Even she.
Agam.—Most dearly welcome to the Greeks, sweet lady.
Nestor.—Our general doth salute you with a kiss.
Ulysses.—Yet is the kindness but particular:
'Twere better she were kissed in general.
Nest.—And very courtly counsel. I'll begin—So much for Nestor.
Achilles.—I'll take that winter from your lips, fair lady. Achilles bids you welcome
Menelaus.—I had good argument for kissing once.
Patroclus.—But that's no argument for kissing now:
For thus popp'd Paris in his hardiness;
And parted thus you and your argument.
Ulyss.—O deadly gall, and theme of all our scorns!
For which we lose our heads, to gild his horns.
Patr.—The first was Menelaus' kiss;—this mine;
Patroclus kisses you.
Men.— O, this is trim!
Patr.—Paris, and I, kiss evermore for him.
Men.—I'll have my kiss, sir;—Lady, by your leave.
Cressida.—In kissing do you render or receive?
Patr.—Both take and give.
Cress.— I'll make my match to live,
The kiss you take is better than you give;
Therefore no kiss.

Men.—I'll give you boot, I'll give you three for one.
Cress.—You're an odd man; give even or give none.
Men.—An odd man, lady? every man is odd.
Cress.—No, Paris is not; for you know, 'tis true
That you are odd, and he is even with you.
Men.—You fillip me o' the head.
Cress.— No, I'll be sworn.
Ulyss.—It were no match, your nail against his horn.
May I, sweet lady, beg a kiss of you?
Cress.—You may.
Ulyss.— I do desire it.
Cress.— Why, beg then.
Ulyss.—Why then, for Venus' sake, give me a kiss,
When Helen is a maid again, and his.
Cress.—I am your debtor, claim it when 'tis due.
Ulyss.—Never's my day, and then a kiss of you."
TROILUS AND CRESSIDA, act iv. sc. 5.

"I kiss'd it:
I hope it be not gone to tell my lord
That I kiss aught but he."
CYMBELINE, act ii. sc. 3.

". . thus kiss'd he me
As if he pluck'd up kisses by the roots."
OTHELLO, act iii. sc. 4.

"The swiftest harts have posted you by land;
And winds of all the corners kissed your sails
To make your vessel nimble."
CYMBELINE, act ii. sc. 4.

"So sweet a kiss the golden sun gives not
  To those fresh morning drops upon the rose,
As thy eye-beams, when their fresh rays have smote
  The night of dew that on my cheeks down flows."
                              LOVE'S LABOUR LOST, act iv. sc. 2.

"   .   .   the ladies call him sweet;
The stairs, as he treads on them, kiss his feet."
                              LOVE'S LABOUR LOST, act v. sc. 2.

"Sir, I have foretold you then what would ensue:
My prophecy is but half his journey yet;

For yonder walls, that pertly front your town,
Yon towers, whose wanton tops do buss the clouds,
Must kiss their own feet."
                              TROILUS AND CRESSIDA, act iv. sc. 5.

"*Rosalind.*—And his kissing is as full of sanctity as the touch of holy bread.

Celia.—He hath bought a pair of cast lips of Diana: A nun of winter's sisterhood kisses not more religiously; the very ice of chastity is in them."

AS YOU LIKE IT, act iii. sc. 4.

"To bear my lady's train; lest the base earth
Should from the vesture chanced to steal a kiss,
And, of so great a favour growing proud,
Disdain to root the summer-swelling flower,
And make rough winter everlastingly."

TWO GENTLEMEN OF VERONA, act ii. sc. 4.

"Tell them your feats; while they with joyful tears
Wash the congealment from your wounds, and kiss
The honour'd gashes whole."

ANTONY AND CLEOPATRA, act iv. sc. 8.

"And yet not cloy thy lips with loath'd satiety,
   But rather famish them amid their plenty,
Making them red and pale with fresh variety,
   Ten kisses short as one, one long as twenty:
A summer's day will seem an hour but short,
Being wasted in such time-beguiling sport."

"Thou art no man, though of a man's complexion,
For men will kiss even by their own direction."

"Some there be that shadow's kiss:
   Such have but a shadows bliss."

"Her lips to mine how often hath she join'd;
   Between each kiss her oaths of true love swearing.'

" Even so she kiss'd his brow, his cheek, his chin,
And where she ends, she doth anew begin."

" Pure lips, sweet seals in my soft lips imprinted,
    What bargains may I make, still to be sealing?
To sell myself I can be well contented,
    So thou wilt buy, and pay, and use good dealing;
Which purchase if thou make, for fear of slips,
Set thy seal-manual on my wax-red lips.

A thousand kisses buys my heart from me;
    And pay them at thy leisure, one by one.
What is ten hundred touches unto thee?
    Are they not quickly told, and quickly gone?
Say, for non-payment that the debt should double
Is twenty hundred kisses such a trouble?"

" Give me one kiss, I'll give it thee again,
And one for interest, if thou wilt have twain."

" Here come and sit, where never serpent hisses
And being set, I'll smother thee with kisses."

" But when her lips were ready for his pay,
He winks, and turns his head another way."
VENUS AND ADONIS.

" I dreamt my lady came and found me dead;
(Strange dream, that gives a dead man leave to think!)
And breath'd such life with kisses in my lips
That I reviv'd, and was an emperor."
ROMEO AND JULIET, act v. sc. 1.

"And lips, O you
The doors of breath, seal with a righteous kiss."
  ROMEO AND JULIET, act v. sc. 3.

"This is a soldier's kiss."
  ANTONY AND CLEOPATRA, act iv. sc. 4.

"The ruddiness upon her lip is wet;
You'll mar it, if you kiss it; stain your own
With oily painting."
  WINTER'S TALE, act v. sc. 3.

"Just as I do now,
He would kiss you twenty with a breath."

"Bear her my true love's kiss, and so, farewell."

" *Romeo.*—If I profane with my unworthy hand
This holy shrine, the gentle fine is this—
My lips, two blushing pilgrims, ready stand
  To smooth that rough touch with a tender kiss.
  Juliet.—Good pilgrim, you do wrong your hand too much.
Which mannerly devotion shows in this;
For saints have hands that pilgrims' hands do touch,
  And palm to palm is holy palmers' kiss.
  Romeo.—Have not saints lips, and holy palmers too?

  Juliet.—Ay, pilgrim, lips that they must use in prayer.
  Romeo.—O then, dear saint, let lips do what hands do;
    They pray, grant thou, lest faith turn to despair.
  Juliet.—Saints do not move, though grant for prayers' sake.
  Romeo.—Then move not, while my prayers' effect I take.
Thus from my lips, by thine my sin is purg'd
                              [*kissing her*].
  Juliet.—Then have my lips the sin that they have took.

Romeo.—Sin from my lips? O trespass sweetly urg'd! Give me my sin again.
Juliet.—You kiss by the book."
ROMEO AND JULIET, act i. sc. 5.

" 'Tis time to fear when tyrants seem to kiss."
PERICLES, act i. sc. 2.

" Is't night's predominance, or the day's shame,
That darkness does the face of earth intomb,
When living light should kiss it?"
MACBETH, act ii. sc. 4.

" O, take this warm kiss on thy pale cold lips."
TITUS ANDRONICUS, act v. sc. 3.

"You that choose not by the view,
  Chance as fair, and choose as true!
Since this fortune falls to you,
  Be content, and seek no new.
If you be well pleas'd with this,
  And hold your fortune for your bliss,
Turn you where your lady is
  And claim her with a loving kiss."

"And, that I love the tree from whence thou sprang'st,
Witness the loving kiss I give the fruit:—
(To say the truth, so Judas kiss'd his master;
And cried—all hail! when as he meant—all harm!")
3 HENRY VI., act v. sc. 7.

"Play the maid's part; still answer nay, and take it."
RICHARD III., act iii. sc. 7.

"I will kiss thy lips—
Haply, some poison yet doth hang on them
To make me die with a restorative."
ROMEO AND JULIET, act v. sc. 3.

"Bear her my true love's kiss, and so, farewell."
RICHARD III., act iv. sc. 5.

"Boys are not to kiss."
ALL'S WELL THAT ENDS WELL, act iv. sc. 3.

"And steal immortal blessings from her lips;
Who, even in pure and vestal modesty,
Still blush, as thinking their own kisses sin."
ROMEO AND JULIET, act iii. sc. 3.

"How oft, when thou, my music, music play'st,
    Upon that blessed wood whose motion sounds
With thy sweet fingers, when thou gently sway'st
    The wiry concord that mine ear confounds,
Do I envy those jacks, that nimble leap
    To kiss the tender inward of thy hand
Whilst my poor lips, which should that harvest-reap,
    At the wood's boldness by thee blushing stand!
To be so tickled, they would change their state
    And situation with those dancing chips,
O'er whom thy fingers walk with gentle gait,
    Making dead wood more bless'd than living lips.
    Since saucy jacks so happy are in this,
    Give them thy fingers, me thy lips to kiss."
SONNET 128.

"But if thou fall, O then imagine this
　　The earth, in love with thee, thy footing trips,
　And all is but to rob thee of a kiss!"

VENUS AND ADONIS.

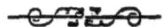

Lord Byron.

"A LONG, long kiss, a kiss of youth, and love
 And beauty, all concentrating like rays
Into one focus, kindled from above;
 Such kisses as belong to early days
 Where heart, and soul, and sense in concert
And the blood's lava, and the pulse a blaze,   [move,
Each kiss a heart quake,—for a kiss's strength,
I think, it must be reckon'd by its length."

"Such kisses as belong to early days."

" 'Tis pleasing to be school'd in a strange tongue
 By female lips and eyes—that is, I mean,
When both the teacher and the taught are young
 As was the case, at least, where I have been;

They smile so when one's right, and when one's wrong
  They smile still more, and then there intervene
Pressure of hands, perhaps even a chaste kiss;—
  I learn'd the little that I know by this."

"'Kiss' rhymes to 'bliss' in fact as well as verse—
I wish it never led to something worse."

"   . . . She press'd
His lips to hers, and silenc'd him with this,
And then dismiss'd the omen from her breast,
Defying augury with that fond kiss."

"When we two parted
    In silence and tears,
Half broken-hearted
    To sever for years,

Pale grew thy cheek and cold,
　　Colder thy kiss:
Truly that hour foretold
　　Sorrow to this."

　　　　" —by God's blessing
With youth and health all kisses are heaven-kissing."

"The First Kiss of Love.

Away with your fictions of flimsy romance;
　　Those tissues of falsehood which folly has wove!
Give me the mild beam of the soul-breathing glance,
　　Or the rapture which dwells on the first kiss of love.

Ye rhymers, whose bosoms with fantasy glow,
　　Whose pastoral passions are made for the grove;
From what blest inspiration your sonnets would flow,
　　Could you ever have tasted the first kiss of love. !

If Apollo should e'er his assistance refuse,
    Or the Nine be disposed from your service to rove,
Invoke them no more, bid adieu to the muse,
    And try the effect of the first kiss of love!

I hate you, ye cold compositions of art!
    Though prudes may condemn me, and bigots reprove,
I court the effusions that spring from the heart,
    Which throbs with delight to the first kiss of love!

Your shepherds, your flocks, those fantastical themes,
    Perhaps may amuse, yet they never can move:
Arcadia displays but a region of dreams;
    What are visions like these to the first kiss of love?

Oh! cease to affirm that man, since his birth,
    From Adam till now, has with wretchedness strove;
Some portion of paradise still is on earth,
    And Eden revives in the first kiss of love.

When age chills the blood, when our pleasures are past—
    For years fleet away with the wings of the dove—
The dearest remembrance will still be the last,
    Our sweetest memorial, the first kiss of love."

"To Ellen.

Oh! might I kiss those eyes of fire,
A million scarce would quench desire:
Still would I steep my lips in bliss,
And dwell an age on every kiss:

Nor then my soul should sated be ;
Still would I kiss and cling to thee :
Nought should my kiss from thine dissever ;
Still would we kiss, and kiss for ever ;
E'en though the numbers did exceed
The yellow harvest's countless seed.
To part would be a vain endeavour :
Could I desist ?—ah ! never—never !"

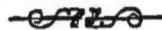

Tom Moore.

"THE kiss that she left on my lip,
    Like a dewdrop shall lingering lie;
'Twas nectar she gave me to sip;
    'Twas nectar I drank in her sigh.

The dew that distill'd in that kiss,
    To my soul was voluptuous wine:
Ever since it is drunk with the bliss,
    And feels a delirium divine."

" When infant bliss in roses slept,
    Cupid upon his slumbers crept,

And while a balmy sigh he stole,
Exhaling from the infant's soul,
He smiling said, 'With this, with this,
I'll send my Julia's burning kiss.' "

" Sweetly you kiss, my Lais dear!
But, while you kiss, I feel a tear,
Bitter, as those when lovers part,
In mystery from your eyelid start!
Sadly you lean your head to mine,
And round my neck in silence twine,
Your hair along my bosom spread,
All humid with the tears you shed!
Have I not kissed those lids of snow?
Yet still, my love, like founts they flow,
Bathing our cheeks, whene'er they meet—
Why is it thus? do tell me, sweet!
Ah! Lais, are my bodings right?
Am I to lose you? is to-night
Our last?—go, false to heaven and me,
Your very tears are treachery."

" While she stole thro' the garden, where heart's ease was
    growing,
  She cull'd some, and kiss'd off its night-fallen dew;
And a rose further on looked so tempting and glowing,
  That, spite of her haste, she must gather it too;

But while o'er the roses too carelessly leaning
    Her zone flew in two and the heart's ease was lost:
'Ah! this means,' said the girl (and she sigh'd at its meaning),
    ' That love is scarce worth the repose it will cost.' "

"If you'd Let Me!

I ne'er on that lip for a minute have gazed
    But a thousand temptations beset me,
And I've thought, as the dear little rubies you raised,
    How delicious 'twould be—if you'd let me!

Then be not so angry for what I have done,
    Nor say that you've sworn to forget me;
They were buds of temptation too pouting to shun,
    And I thought that—you could not but let me!

When your lip with a whisper came close to my cheek,
   O think how bewitching it met me!
And plain as the eye of a Venus could speak,
   Your eye seemed to say—you would let me!
Then forgive the transgression and bid me remain,
   For in truth, if I go, you'll regret me;
Or, oh! let me try the transgression again,
   And I'll do all you wish—will you let me?'"

"Rondeau.

'Good night!' 'Good night!'—and is it so?
And must I from my Rosa go?
Oh, Rosa! say 'Good night!' once more,
And I'll repeat it o'er and o'er,
Till the first glance of dawning light
Shall find us saying still 'Good night.'

And still 'Good night!' my Rosa, say—
But whisper still, 'A minute stay;'
And I will stay, and every minute
Shall have an age of rapture in it,
We'll kiss and kiss in quick delight
And murmur, while we kiss, 'Good night!'

'Good night!' you'll murmur with a sigh,
And tell me it is time to fly;
And I will vow to kiss no more,
And kiss you closer than before;—
Till slumber seal our weary sight—
And then, my love! my soul! 'Good night!'"

"When your lip has met mine in abandonment sweet,
 Have we felt as if virtue forbid it?
Have we felt as if Heaven denied them to meet?
 No, rather 'twas Heaven that did it!

So innocent, love! is the pleasure we sip,
 So little of guilt is there in it,
That I wish all my errors were lodged on your lip,
 And I'd steal them away in a minute!"

———

"My kisses have not stained the rose
 Which Nature hung upon your lip;
And still your sigh with nectar flows
 For many a raptured soul to sip.

Farewell! and when some other fair
 Shall call your wanderer to her arms,
'Twill be my luxury to compare
 Her spells with your remembered charms!

'This cheek,' I'll say, 'is not so bright,
 As one that used to meet my kiss;
This eye has not such liquid light
 As one that used to talk of bliss!'"

———

"'I never give a kiss,' says Prue,
 'To naughty man, for I abhor it.'
She will not *give* a kiss 'tis true,
 She'll *take* one though, and thank you for it!"

"Old Cloe, whose withering kisses
    Have long set the loves at defiance,
Now, done with the science of blisses
    May fly to the blisses of science!"

"How heavenly was the poet's doom,
    To breathe his spirit through a kiss;
And lose within so sweet a tomb,
    The trembling messenger of bliss!

And, ah! his soul returned to feel
    That it *again* could ravished be;
For in the kiss that thou didst steal,
    His life and soul have fled to thee!"

"Her lip!—oh, call me not false-hearted,
    When such a lip I fondly pressed;

'Twas Love some melting cherry parted,
   Gave thee one half and her the rest!

And when, with all thy murmuring tone
   They sued, half open, to be kissed,
I could as soon resist thine own—
   And them, Heaven knows! I ne'er resist!"

"The Kiss.

Grow to my lips, thou sacred kiss,
On which my soul's beloved swore,
That there should come a time of bliss,
When she would mock my hopes no more;
And fancy shall thy glow renew,
In sighs at morn, and dreams at night,
And none shall steal thy holy dew
Till thou'rt absolv'd by rapture's rite;
Sweet hours that are to make me bless'd,
Oh! fly, like breezes, to the goal,
And let my love, my more than soul,
Come panting to this fever'd breast:
And while in every glance I drink
The rich o'erflowings of her mind,
Oh! let her all impassioned sink,
In sweet abandonment resign'd,
Blushing for all our struggles past,
And murmuring, 'I am thine at last!'"

"Thou weep'st for me—do weep—oh! that I durst
Kiss off that tear! but, no—these lips are curst,
They must not touch thee;—one divine caress,
One blessed moment of forgetfulness
I've had within those arms, and *that* shall lie
Shrin'd in my soul's deep memory till I die."
LALLAH ROOKH.

Faithless.

"Take back the sigh, thy lips of art
    In passion's moment breath'd to me,
Yet, no—it must not, will not part,
'Tis now the life breath of my heart,
    And has become too pure for thee.

Take back the kiss, that faithless sigh,
    With all the warmth of truth imprest;
Yet, no—the fatal kiss may lie.
Upon thy lips its sweets would die,
    Or bloom to make a rival blest.

Take back the vows that, night and day,
    My heart receiv'd, I thought, from thine,
Yet, no—allow them still to stay,
They might some other heart betray,
    As sweetly as they've ruin'd mine."

A Kiss à l'Antique.

"Behold, my love, the curious gem
    Within this simple ring of gold;

'Tis hallowed by the touch of them
    Who lived in classic hours of old.

Some fair Athenian girl, perhaps,
    Upon her hand this gem display'd,
Nor thought that Time's eternal lapse
    Should see it grace a lovelier maid.

Look, darling, what a sweet design!
    The more we gaze, it charms the more;
Come,—closer bring that cheek to mine,
    And trace with me its beauties o'er.

Thou see'st it is a simple youth
    By some enamoured nymph embraced;
Look, Nea, love, and say in sooth
    Is not her hand most dearly placed?

Upon his curly head behind
    It seems in careless play to lie,
Yet presses gently, half inclined
    To bring his lips of nectar nigh.

Oh! happy maid, too happy boy;
    The one so fond and faintly loth,
The other yielding slow to joy—
    Oh! rare indeed, but blissful both.

Imagine, love, that I am he,
    And just as warm as he is chilling;
Imagine, too, that thou art she,
    But quite as cold as she is willing.

So may we try the graceful way
    In which their gentle arms are twined,

And thus, like her, my hand I lay
    Upon thy wreath'd hair behind,

And thus I feel thee breathing sweet,
    As slow to mine thy head I move!
And thus our lips together meet,
    And—thus I kiss thee—oh, my love.'

''Tis sweet to Think.

'Tis sweet to think, that, where'er we rove,
    We are sure to find something blissful and dear,
And that, when we're far from the lips we love,
    We've but to make love to the lips that are near!

The heart, like a tendril, accustom'd to cling,
    Let it grow where it will, cannot flourish alone,

But will lean to the nearest and lovliest thing
    It can twine in itself, and make closely its own.

Then oh! what pleasure, where'er we rove,
    To be sure to find something, still that is dear,
And to know, when far from the lips we love,
    We've but to make love to the lips we are near.
'Twere a shame, when flowers around us rise,
    To make light of the rest, if the rose isn't there;
And the world's so rich in resplendent eyes,
    'Twere a pity to limit one's love to a pair.

Love's wing and the peacock's are nearly alike,
    They are both of them bright, but they're changeable too!
And wherever a new beam of beauty can strike
    It will tincture Love's plume with a different hue!
Then, oh! what pleasure, where'er we rove,
    To be doom'd to find something, still that is dear,
And to know, when far from the lips we love,
    We have but to make love to the lips we are near."

" Here maidens are sighing, and fragrant their sigh
    As the flower of the Amra just op'd by a bee;
And precious their tears as that rain from the sky,
    Which turns into pearls as it falls in the sea.
Oh! think what the kiss and the smile must be worth
    When the sigh and the tear are so perfect in bliss,
And own if there be an Elysium on earth,
        It is this, it is this." LALLAH ROOKH.

"Oh! let our lips, our cheeks be laid
But near each other while they fade;
Let us but mix our parting breaths,
And I can die ten thousand deaths."
LALLAH ROOKH.

"What the Bee is to the Floweret.

What the bee is to the floweret,
   When he looks for honey dew,
Through the leaves that close embow'r it,
   That, my love, I'll be to you.
What the bank with verdure glowing,
   Is to waves that wander near,
Whisp'ring kisses, while they're going,
   That I'll be to you, my dear.
But they say the bee's a rover,
   That he'll fly when sweets are gone;
And, when once the kiss is over,
   Faithless brooks will wander on!
Nay, if flowers will lose their looks,
   If sunny banks will wear away,
'Tis but right that bees and brooks
   Should sip and kiss them while they may."

"Drink to me only with thine eyes
 And I will pledge with mine;
 Or leave a kiss within the cup,
 And I'll not ask for wine."

"Sweet seducer! blandly smiling,
 Charming still, and still beguiling;
 Oft I swore to love thee never,
 Yet I love thee more than ever.
 Why that little wanton blushing,
 Glancing eye and bosom flushing?
 Flushing warm, and wily glancing,
 All is lovely, all entrancing.
 Turn away those lips of blisses—
 I am poison'd by thy kisses;
 Yet again, ah! turn them to me;
 Ruin's sweet when they undo me.
 Oh! be less, be less enchanting;
 Let some little grace be wanting;
 Let my eyes, when I'm expiring
 Gaze awhile, without admiring."

"Oh! never let him know how deep the brow
He kiss'd at parting is dishonour'd now."
LALLAH ROOKH.

"From the heretic girl of my soul should I fly
 To seek somewhere else a more orthodox kiss?"

Burns.

"To a Kiss.

HUMID seal of soft affections,
    Tend'rest pledge of future bliss,
Dearest tie of young connections,
    Love's first snowdrop, virgin kiss.

Speaking silence, dumb confession,
    Passion's birth, and infants' play,
Dove-like fondness, chaste concession,
    Glowing dawn of brighter day.

Sorrowing joy, adieu's last action
    When ling'ring lips no more must join;
What words can ever speak affection
    So thrilling and sincere as thine!"

"Gin a body meet a body
    Coming through the rye,
Gin a body kiss a body,
    Need a body cry?

Gin a body meet a body
    Coming through the glen,
Gin a body kiss a body,
    Need the world ken?"

"Ae fond Kiss.

Ae fond kiss, and then we sever;
Ae fareweel, and then for ever!
Deep in heart-wrung tears I'll pledge thee,
Warring sighs and groans I'll wage thee.
Who shall say that fortune grieves him
While the Star of Hope she leaves him?
Me, nae cheerfu' twinkle lights me;
Dark despair around benights me.

I'll ne'er blame my partial fancy,
Naething could resist my Nancy;
But to see her, was to love her;
Love but her, and love for ever.
Had we never loved sae kindly,
Had we never loved sae blindly,
Never met or never parted,
We had ne'er been broken-hearted

Fare-thee-weel, thou first and fairest!
Fare-thee-weel, thou best and dearest!
Thine be ilka joy and treasure,
Peace, enjoyment, love, and pleasure!
Ae fond kiss, and then we sever;
Ae fareweel, alas! for ever
Deep in heart-wrung tears I'll pledge thee,
Warring sighs and groans I'll wage thee."

"When in my arms, wi' a' thy charms,
    I clasp my countless treasure,
I seek nae mair o' Heaven to share,
    Than sic a moment's pleasure.

And by thy e'en, sae bonnie blue,
    I swear I'm thine for ever,
And on thy lips I seal my vow,
    And break it shall I never."

"If thou should ask my love,
    Could I deny thee?
If thou would win my love,
    Jamie, come try me!

If thou should kiss me, love,
    Wha could espy thee?
If thou wad be my love,
    Jamie, come try me!"

"Delia.

Fair the face of orient day,
    Fair the tints of op'ning rose;
But fairer still my Delia dawns,
    More lovely far her beauty blows.

Sweet the lark's wild-warbling lay,
    Sweet the tinkling rill to hear;
But, Delia, more delightful still,
    Steal thine accents on mine ear!

The flower-enamour'd busy bee,
    The rosy banquet loves to sip;
Sweet the streamlet's limpid lapse
    To the sun-brown Arab's lips.

But, Delia, on thy balmy lips
    Let me, no vagrant insect, rove!
Oh! let me steal one liquid kiss,
    For, oh! my soul is parch'd with love."

"A man may drink and no be drunk;
    A man may fight and no be slain;
A man may kiss a bonnie lass,
    And aye be welcome back again!"

"The minister kiss'd the fiddler's wife,
    And coulda preach for thinking o't."

"Philly and Willy."

He.
The bee that through the sunny hour
Sips nectar in the opening flower,
Compared wi' my delight is poor,
    Upon the lips o' Philly.

She.
The woodbine in the dewy weet
When evening shades in silence meet,
Is nocht sae fragrant or sae sweet
    As is a kiss o' Willy."

" Heaven spare you lang to kiss the breath
    O' mony flowery simmers."

" Her lips are like the cherries ripe
    That sunny walls from Boreas screen,
They tempt the taste and charm the sight
    And she's twa glancin', sparklin' e'en."

" Oh pale, pale now, those rosy lips
    I aft hae kiss'd sae fondly!
And closed for aye, the sparkling glance
    That dwelt on me sae fondly."

" I'll pu' the budding rose when Phœbus peeps in view,
For it's like a balmy kiss o'er her sweet bonnie mou'."

Tennyson.

"WHAT eyes like thine have waken'd hopes?
What lips like thine so sweetly join'd?
Where on the double rose-bud droops
The fulness of her pensive mind."

"O Love, O fire! once he drew
With one long kiss my whole soul thro'
My lips, as sunlight drinketh dew."

"A man had given all other bliss,
And all his worldly worth for this,
To waste his whole heart on one kiss
Upon her perfect lips."

"But all my heart is drawn above,
   My knees are bow'd in crypt and shrine,
I never felt the kiss of love,
   Nor maiden's hand in mine."

"The Ringlet.

' Your ringlets, your ringlets,
   That look so golden-gay,
If you will give me one, but one,
   To kiss it night and day,
Then never chilling touch of Time
   Will turn it silver-grey;
And then shall I know it is all true gold
To flame and sparkle and stream as of old,
Till all the comets in heaven are cold,
   And all her stars decay.'
' Then take it, love, and put it by;
This cannot change, nor yet can I.'

'My ringlet, my ringlet,
   That art so golden-gay,
Now never chilling touch of Time
   Can turn thee silver-gray;
And a lad may wink, and a girl may hint,
   And a fool may say his say;
For my doubts and fears were all amiss,
And I swear henceforth by this and this,
That a doubt will only come for a kiss,
   And a fear to be kiss'd away.'
'Then kiss it, love, and put it by:
If this can change, why so can I.'

'O ringlet, O ringlet,
   I kiss'd you night and day,
And ringlet, O ringlet,
   You still are golden-gay,
But ringlet, O ringlet,
   You should be silver-gray:
For what is this which now I'm told,
I that took you for true gold?
She that gave you's bought and sold,
        Sold, sold.

'O ringlet, O ringlet,
   She blush'd a rosy red,
When ringlet, O ringlet,
   She clipt you from her head,
And ringlet, O ringlet,
   She gave you me, and said,

'Come, kiss it, love, and put it by:
If this can change, why so can I.'
O fie, you golden nothing, fie,
     You golden lie.

'O ringlet, O ringlet,
 I count you much to blame,
For ringlet, O ringlet,
 You put me much to shame.
So ringlet, O ringlet,
 I doom you to the flame.
For what is this which now I learn,
Has given all my faith a turn?
Burn, you glossy heretic, burn,
     Burn, burn.'"

"The talking Oak.

'But tell me, did she read the name
 I carved with many vows,
When last with throbbing heart I came
 To rest beneath thy boughs?'

'O yes, she wander'd round and round
 These knotted knees of mine,
And found, and kiss'd the name she found,
 And sweetly murmur'd thine.

'A tear-drop trembled from its source,
 And down my surface crept,

My sense of touch is something coarse,
    But I believe she wept.

'Then flush'd her cheek with rosy light,
    She glanced across the plain;
But not a creature was in sight:
    She kiss'd me once again.

'Her kisses were so close and kind,
    That, trust me on my word,
Hard wood I am, and wrinkled rind,
    But yet my sap was stirr'd.'"

"His spirit flutters like a lark,
    He stoops—to kiss her—on his knee,
'Love, if thy tresses be so dark,
    How dark those hidden eyes must be!'"

" ' O eyes long laid in happy sleep.
O happy sleep that lightly fled!
O happy kiss, that woke thy sleep!
O love, thy kiss would wake the dead!' "

" The page has caught her hand in his;
Her lips are sever'd as to speak:
His own are pouted to a kiss:
The blush is fix'd upon her cheek."

"A touch, a kiss! the charm was snapt!"

"As thro' the land at eve we went,
And pluck'd the ripen'd ears,
We fell out, my wife and I,
O we fell out, I know not why,
And kiss'd again with tears.

For when we came where lies the child
    We lost in other years,
There above the little grave,
O there above the little grave,
    We kiss'd again with tears."

" Dear as remember'd kisses after death,
    And sweet as those by hopeless fancy feign'd
On lips that are for others."

" The trance gave way,
To those caresses, when a hundred times
In that last kiss, which never was the last,
Farewell, like endless welcome, lived and died."

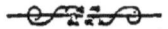

Coleridge.

"To a Kiss.

'ONE kiss, dear maid!' I said, and sigh'd—
'Your scorn the little boon denied.
Ah, why refuse the blameless bliss?
Can danger lurk within a kiss?
Yon viewless wand'rer of the vale,
The Spirit of the Western Gale,
At morning's break, at evening's close
Inhales the sweetness of the rose,
And hovers o'er th' uninjur'd bloom,
Sighing back the sweet perfume,
Vigour to the zephyr's wing
Her nectar-breathing kisses fling;
And he the glitter of the dew
Scatters on the rose's hue.'
Bashful, lo, she bends her head,
And darts a flush of deeper red.

Too well those lovely lips disclose
The triumphs of the op'ning rose;
O fair! O graceful! bid them prove
As passive to the breath of Love.
In tender accents, faint and low,
Well pleas'd, I hear the whisper'd 'No!'

The whisper'd 'No'—how little meant!
Sweet Falsehood, that endears Consent;
For on those lovely lips the while
Dawns the soft relenting smile,
And tempts with feign'd dissuasion coy
The gentle violence of joy."

"The Composition of a Kiss.

Cupid, if storying legends tell aright,
Once framed a rich elixir of delight.
A chalice o'er love-kindled flames he fix'd,
And in it nectar and ambrosia mix'd.
With these the magic dews which evening brings,
Brush'd from the Idalian star by fairy wings;

Each tender pledge of sacred faith he join'd,
Each gentler pleasure of the unspotted mind—

Day dreams, whose tints with sportive blightness glow,
And Hope, the blameless parasite of Woe.
The eyeless chemist heard the process rise,
The steamy chalice bubbled up in sighs;
Sweet sounds transpir'd, as when the enamour'd dove
Pours the soft murm'ring of responsive love.
The finish'd work might Envy vainly blame,
And 'Kisses' was the precious compound's name
With half the god his Cyprian mother blest,
And breath'd on Sara's lovelier lips the rest."

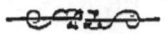

Combe.

"SQUIRE.—This, Doctor Syntax, is my sister:
Why, my good sir, you have not kiss'd her.
    SYNTAX.—Do not suppose, I'm such a brute
As to disdain the sweet salute.
    SQUIRE.—And this, sir, is my loving wife,
The joy and honour of my life.
    SYNTAX.—A lovely lady to the view!
And, with your leave, I'll kiss her too."

" Her warm embraces she renew'd;
While he, delighted, fondly kiss'd
Those hands which, formed into a fist,
Had often warmed his eyes and nose
To turn from their tremendous blows."

" How sweet to wind along the cool retreat,
    To look and gaze on Delia as I go;
To mingle sweet discourse with kisses sweet,
    And teach my lovely scholar all I know."

" With heart of joy and look of woe,
The Doctor now prepar'd to go,
He silent squeez'd the Squire's hands
And ask of madam her commands.

The Squire exclaim'd, 'Why so remiss?
She bids you take a hearty kiss;
And if you think that one won't do,
I beg, dear sir, you'll give her *two:*'
'Nay, then,' said Syntax, 'you shall see!'
And straight he gave the lady *three.*
The lady, blushing, thank'd him too,
And in soft accents said, 'Adieu!'"

Tom Hood.

"OH, for the lessons learned by heart!
　　Ay, though the very birch's smart
　　　　Should mark those hours again;
　　I'd 'kiss the rod,' and be resigned,
　　Beneath the stroke, and even find
　　　　Some sugar in the cane."

" He took the hint full speedily, and, back'd
　　By love, and night, and the occasion's meetness,
Bestowed a something on her cheek that smack'd
　　(Though quite in silence) of ambrosial sweetness,
That made her think all other kisses lacked
　　Till then, but what, she knew not, of completeness:
Being used but sisterly salutes to feel,—
Insipid things, like sandwiches of veal."

" O happy, happy, thrice happy state,
　　When such a bright planet governs the fate
　　　　Of a pair of united lovers!
　　'Tis theirs, in spite of the serpent's hiss,
　　To enjoy the pure primeval kiss
　　With as much of the old original bliss
　　　　As mortality ever recovers!"

Stanley.

"WHEN on thy lips my soul I breathe,
    Which there meets thine;
Freed from their fetters by that death,
    Our subtle forms combine:
Thus without bonds of sense they move,
And like two cherubims converse by love.

    Spirits, to chains of death confin'd,
        Converse by sense;
    But ours, that are by flames refin'd,
        With those weak ties dispense:
Let such in words their minds display,
We in a kiss our mutual thoughts convey.

    But since my soul from me doth fly,
        To thee retir'd,
    Thou canst not both retain, for I
        Must be by one inspir'd:
Then, dearest, either justly mine
Restore, or in exchange let me have thine.

    Yet if thou dost return mine own,
        Oh! tak't again!
    For 'tis this pleasing death alone
        Gives ease unto my pain:
Kill me once more, or I shall find
Thy pity than thy cruelty less kind."

"Rosa.

Oh! Rosa, I have never felt
    Till now, the bliss of wooing,
Or known how soon the soul could melt
    With rapture, love, and ruin.

But you, bewitching girl! have taught
    My soul to woo sincerely,
And you have robb'd that soul of aught
    It yet had valued dearly.

The kiss you gave the other night,
    Though full of woe and anguish,
Was one for whose intense delight
    My soul in pain could languish.

And keener as the torment grew
    That kiss would sure be sweeter;
And faster, as my reason flew,
    Its throbbing joy completer.

Until, confounded with the bliss
    We turn'd awhile to sorrow
Resolv'd to taste another kiss
    Of equal warmth to-morrow.

Oh! not to-morrow, but to-night
    Let us again indulge it;
And by yon moon's auspicious light
    I swear not to divulge it.

And if, like yonder moon, my fair
   Grow larger, lovelier, brighter,
With many a warmer kiss I swear
   In future to delight her.

Then each inspired kiss imparts,
   In sounds, half utter'd, half suppress'd,
The tender secrets of their hearts,
   Secrets to lips alone confess'd.

Where soul is thus with soul entwined,
   The living rapture is improved;
'Tis rapture of the sweetest kind,
   To kiss when kiss'd, to love when loved."

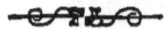

Leigh Hunt

"JENNY kiss'd me when we met,
   Jumping from the chair she sat in,
Time, you thief, who love to get
   Sweets upon your list, put that in;
Say I'm weary, say I'm sad,
   Say that health and wealth have miss'd me,
Say I'm growing old,—but add—
       Jenny kiss'd me!"

Drummond.

"THOUGH I, with strange desire
    To kiss those lips am set on fire,
  Yet will I cease to crave
    Sweet kisses in such store
    As he who long before
In thousands them from Lesbia did receive;
    Sweetheart, but once me kiss,
    And I, by that sweet bliss,
E'en swear to cease you to importune more:
    Poor one, no number is—
Another word of me you shall not hear
After one kiss, but still one kiss, my dear!"

"Dear life, when I do touch
    Those coral ports of bliss,
    Which still themselves do kiss—
And sweetly me invite to do as much;
All panting on thy lips
    My heart my life doth leave,
    Nor sense my senses have,
And inward powers do feel a strange eclipse;
    This death so heavenly well
    Doth me so please, that I
Would never longer seek in sense to dwell,
If that e'er thus I only could but die."

Beaumont and Fletcher.

"TAKE, ah! take those lips away,
    That so sweetly were forsworn,
And those eyes, the break of day,
    Lights that do mislead the morn;
But my kisses bring again
Seals of love, but seal'd in vain.

Hide, oh! hide those hills of snow,
    Which thy frozen bosom bears;
On whose tops the pinks that grow
    Are of those which April wears,
But my poor heart, oh! first set free,
Bound in those icy chains by thee."

"Humid seal of soft affection,
    Tend'rest pledge of future bliss;
Dearest tie of young connection,
    Love's first snowdrop, virgin kiss.

Speaking silence! dumb confession!
    Passion's birth and infants' play,
Dove-like fondness, chaste concession,
    Glowing dawn of brighter day.

Sorrowing joy! adieu's last action,
    When ling'ring lips no more must join;
What words can ever speak affection
    So thrilling, so sincere as thine!

Thee the fond youth untaught and simple
    Nor on the naked breast can find,
Nor within the cheek's small dimple—
    Sole offspring thou of lips conjoin'd.

Then haste thee to thy dewy mansion,
    With Hebe spend thy laughing day;
Dwell in her rubied lips' expansion,
    Bask in her eye's propitious ray."

"So I left this young Sappho, and hasten'd to fly
    To those sweeter logicians in bliss,
Who argue the point with a soul-telling eye,
    And convince us at once with a kiss."

Ben Jonson.

"FOR love's sake kiss me once again,
I long, and should not beg in vain,
There's none to spy or see;
Why do you doubt or stay?
I'll taste as lightly as the bee
That doth but touch his flower, and fly away

Once more, and, faith, I will be gone,
Can he that loves take less than one?
Nay, you may err in this,
And all your bounty wrong;
This could be called but half a kiss,
What we're to do but once, we should do long.

I will but mend the last, and tell
Where now it would have relish'd well;
Join lip to lip and try,
Each suck other's breath,
And whilst our tongues perplexed lie
Let who will think us dead, or wish our death."

" The parting kiss, the soft embrace,
I feel them at my heart!
'Twas joy to clasp you in these arms,
But agony to part.

Yet let us tranquillise our minds,
And hope the time may be,
When I shall see that face again,
So lov'd, so dear to me."

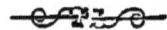

Stephens.

"YE delicate lovelies, with leave I maintain
    That happiness here you must find;
To yourselves I appeal for felicity's reign,
    When you meet with a man to your mind.

When gratitude friendship to fondness unites,
    Inexpressive endearments arise;
Then hopes, fears, and fancies, strange doubts and delights
    Are announced by those tell-tale eyes.

Those technical terms in the science of love
    Cold schoolmen attempt to describe,
But how should they paint what they never can prove?
    For tenderness knows not their tribe!

Of all the abuse on enjoyment that's thrown,
    The treatment love takes most amiss,
Is the rant of the coxcomb, the sot, and the clown,
    Who pretend to indulge in a kiss.

In circling embraces, when lips to lips move,
    Description, oh! teach me to praise
The overture kiss to the opera of love—
    But beauty would laugh at the phrase.

Love's preludes are kisses, and, after the play,
    They fill up the pause of delight;

The rich repetitions, which never decay
    The lips' silent language at night.

The rapture of kissing we only can taste,
    When sympathies equal inspire;
And while to enjoyment unbounded we haste,
    Their breath blows the coals of desire.

Again, and again, and again, beauty sips,
    When feeling these pressures excite;
When fleeting life's stopp'd by a kiss of the lips,
    Then sinks in a flood of delight."

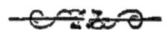

Peter Pindar.

"HEN we dwell on the lips of the lass we adore,
    Not a pleasure in nature is missing;
May his soul be in heav'n, he deserv'd it, I'm sure,
    Who was first the inventor of kissing.

Master Adam, I verily think, was the man,
    Whose discovery will ne'er be surpass'd;
Well, since the sweet game with creation began,
    To the end of the world may it last."

"For soon I led the yielding fair
By gentlest words, and tend'rest care,
From granting first a sidelong kiss,
To the more dear delightful bliss,
With which the melting soul's replete
When lips meet lips in kisses sweet!"

"'I'll scream if you touch me!'
Exclaimed a pert miss,
Whose lover was seeking
An innocent kiss.

By this prudish conduct
Cold water was thrown;
The lover drew backward
And let her alone.

'I'll scream if you touch me!'
　　She holler'd once more;
He cried, 'I aint near you!'
　　And turned on the shore.

She quickly subsided,
　　Grew tender to view,
And whisper'd quite softly—
　　'I'll scream till you do!'"

"I dare not ask a kiss,
　　I dare not beg a smile,
Lest, having that or this,
　　I might grow proud the while.

No, no; the utmost share
    Of my desire shall be,
As I now kiss the air,
    It may be borne to thee."

Kents.

"JUST so may love, although 'tis understood
The mere commingling of passionate breath,
Produce more than our searching witnesseth;
What I know not; but who, of men, can tell
That flowers would bloom, or that green fruit would swell
To melting pulp, that fish would have bright mail,
The earth its dower of rivers, wood, and vale,
The meadows runnels, runnels pebble-stones,
The seed its harvest, or the lute its tones,
Tones ravishment, or ravishment its sweet,
If human souls did never kiss and greet."

"Now a soft kiss—
Ay, by that kiss, I vow an endless bliss,
An immortality of passion's thine."

"Echo hence shall stir
No sighs but sigh-warm kisses."

"Like the hid scent in an unbudded rose—
Ay, a sweet kiss."

"Catch the white-handed nymphs in shady places
To woo sweet kisses from averted faces."

"Straight he seized her wrist,
It melted from his grasp; her hand he kiss'd,
And, horror! kiss'd his own—he was alone!"

"My Indian bliss!
My river-lily bud! one human kiss."

H. Kirke White.

"Oh! I would walk
A weary journey to the farthest verge
Of the big world, to kiss that good man's hand,
Who, in the blaze of wisdom and of art,
Preserves a lowly mind!"

"Happy is he, who, though the cup of bliss
Has ever shunn'd him when he thought to kiss;
Who, still in abject poverty or pain,
Can count with pleasure what small joys remain."

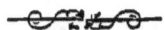

Shelley.

"STAY yet awhile! speak to me once again;
 Kiss me, so long but as a kiss may live; -
 And in my heartless breast and burning brain
 That word, that kiss, shall all thoughts else survive,
 With food of saddest memory kept alive."

"Sleep, the fresh dew of languid love, the rain
 Whose drops quench kisses till they burn again."

"A sensitive plant in a garden grew,
 And the young winds fed it with silver dew,
 And it opened its fan-like leaves to the light,
 And closed them beneath the kisses of night."

"But the bee, and the beamlike ephemeris,
 Whose path is the lightning's, and soft moth that kiss
 The sweet lips of the flowers, and harm not."

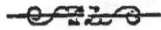

Garrick.

"FOR me my fair a wreath has wove,
    Where rival flow'rs in union meet;
As oft she kiss'd the gift of love,
    Her breath gave sweetness to the sweet.

A bee within a damask rose
    Had crept, the nectar'd dew to sip;
But lesser sweets the thief foregoes—
    And fixes on Louisa's lip.

There tasting all the bloom of spring
    Wak'd by the ripening breath of May
Th' ungrateful spoiler left his sting
    And with the honey flew away."

"When zephyr on the violet blows,
    Or breathes upon the damask rose,

He does not half the sweets disclose
    That does my lovely Peggy.

I stole a kiss the other day,
And, trust me, naught but truth I say,
The fragrance of the blooming May
  Is not so sweet as Peggy."

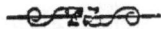

Aaron Hill.

"AURELIA, thou art mine!' I cried; and she
Sigh'd soft, 'Now, Damon, thou art lord of me!'
'But wilt thou,' whisper'd she, 'the knot now tied,
Which only death's keen weapon can divide,
Wilt thou, still mindful of thy raptures past,
Permit the summer of love's hope to last?
Shall not cold wintry frosts come on too soon?
Ah, say! what means the world by honey-moon?
If we so short a space our bliss enjoy,
What toils does love for one poor month employ?'
'Lest more,' said I, 'thou shouldst profane the bliss
I'll seal thy dang'rous lips with this close kiss;
Nor thus the heav'n of marriage hopes blaspheme,
But learn from me to speak on this lov'd theme,
There have been wedlock joys of swift decay
Like lightning, seen at once, and shot away;
But theirs were hopes, which, all unfit to pair,
Like fire and powder, kiss'd, and flash'd to air!
Thy soul and mine, by mutual courtship won,
Meet like two mingling flames, and make but one,
Union of hearts, nor hands, does marriage make;
'Tis sympathy of minds keeps love awake.
Our growing days increase of joy shall know,
And thick-sown comforts leave no room for woe.

Thou, the soft-swelling vine, shalt fruitful last,
I, the strong elm, will prop thy beauty fast;
Thou shalt strew sweets to soften life's rough way
And, when hot passions my proud wishes sway,
Thou, like some breeze, shalt in my bosom play.
Thou, for protection, shalt on me depend,
I, find in thee a soft and faithful friend;
I, in Aurelia, shall for ever view
At once my care, my fear, my comfort too;
Thou shalt first partner in my pleasures be,
But all my pains shall, last, be known to thee.'
Aurelia heard, and view'd me with a smile,
Which seem'd at once to cherish and revile;
'O, god of love!' she cried, ' what joys were thine,
If all life's race were wedding days like mine!'"

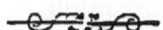

Various Authors.

The Mistletoe.

"HEY! for the mistletoe!
 Trip it, and twistle toe!
  I prithee, young miss
  A dance and a kiss,
The season shall be your immunity.
 Say 'yes' to the dance,
 And off with a glance
  That leaves all the rest,
  To your partner when best
Occasion shall give opportunity!

 What now? Hesitation!
 Then hear my narration,
  That'll prove to you how,
  'Neath the mistletoe bough,
Your duty at Christmas to kiss is;
 How girls that refuse
 Their lovers shall lose,
  And always regretting
  Their foolish coquetting,
Remain everlastingly—misses!

When the British warrior queen
 (Ere she heard of Roman rods)—

Sought one day with pensive mien,
    Counsel from Sir Thomas Dods.

Sage beneath a spreading oak
    Sat that Druid hoary chief,
Every solemn word he spoke
    Gaining from her quick belief.

She had told that her about
    Suitors swarmed of every kind,
And her heart was quite in doubt,
    Which way to make up her mind.

' Tell me, Dods, how I'm to know
    Which are lovers of my pelf,
Which aspire to consort's show,
    Which one loves me for myself ! '

' Maiden Queen ! our isle's defender !
    See, above us in the tree,
Grows the bane of each pretender ;
    Take this sprig I give to thee.

And when any ardent wooer,
    Makes his last appeal to thee,
You can tell which is the truer,
    And your lover's motive see.

As he lowly bends before you,
    Pouring forth his tale of love,
Swearing how he doth adore you—
    Gently wave this spray above.

This shall help you to discover
  Whether truth is in his prayer;
Show you if an honest lover
  Or a lying knave be there!'

Came then many a lordly prince
  Making love with clam'rous vow,
But sudden each began to wince—
  Falt'ring spoke with puzzled brow.

The queen had gently waved the spray,
  Which stopped the feigned anguish—
The melting words did frozen stay,
  The earnest prayer did languish.

At last there came a gentle youth,
  Who knelt in sad confusion,
His tongue refused to tell his truth
  His tale had no conclusion.

The queen held out the spray above
  And then with sudden rush,
There came the tale of true, true love,
  With proper force and gush.

She married him, and many years
  They reigned side by side—
The court was all aswim with tears
  The day he gently died.

And then the queeen did make a law,
  By which you still are bound,

Your wretched fate shall all deplore
    If breaking it you're found!

'*Ourselves, whereas* the mistletoe
    Hath lent us timely aid,
Let every girl our mandate know,
    And listen every maid!

What time the snow is on the ground
    Hang up this plant with care,
And after dancing it around
    Salute your sweetheart there.

And further learn, that she who won't
    Shall always be a—spinster!
Given this day, at Oidubront—
    (The Saxon for Westminster.)'"

"The Mistletoe,

WHOE'ER is kiss'd beneath my shade,
    Widow, wife, or artless maid,
    And culls my fruit to search my heart,
    And place it next her counterpart,
  True shall her ardent wishes at the moment
Foster'd to life, like me, upon the plant I love.   [prove,
  Should they by fate be grafted on
  The hazel, crab, or prickly thorn,

Tasteless, or soon degen'rate, wild,
With cares beset, with tears beguil'd,
Partaking of the nature where they hapless grow,
She'll rue the baleful plant, the mystic mistletoe."

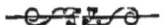

"AH, no! the oak her wishes bear,
The nymph by tender love led there;
Come, then, in Christmas gambols play,
And dance the midnight hours away;
And join in song the warbling lute,
And gather kisses with my fruit;
Let her fond bosom still with mutual rapture glow—
She'll bless the evergreen, the sacred mistletoe."

"GODDESS! I do love a girl
    Ruby lipp'd and tooth'd with pearl,
    If so be I may but prove,
    Lucky in this maid I love,
    I will promise there shall be
Myrtles offered up to thee."

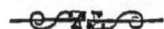

"Let Me Kiss Him for his Mother.

LET me kiss him for his mother,
    Let me kiss his youthful brow;
I will love him for his mother,
    And seek her blessing now.
Kind friends have soothed his pillow—
    Have watch'd his ev'ry care;
Beneath the weeping willow
    Oh! lay him gently there!

Let me kiss him for his mother;
    What tho' left a stranger here,
She has lov'd him as none other:
    I feel her blessing near.
Tho' cold that form lies sleeping,
    Sweet angels watch around,
Dear friends around are weeping,
    O! lay him gently down!"

Modesty.

"'KISS me, dear maid, to seal the vow
    Of love that thou hast made.'
'I have no *right* to kiss thee now,'
    The modest maiden said.

'If thou canst find it in thine heart
    My first wish to refuse,
Perhaps 'tis best that we should part
    Ere we our freedom lose.'

'Although to kiss *you* I demur,
    Yet please to recollect
That if you choose to kiss *me*, sir,
    Of course I—can't object.'"

"Rings and Seals.

'GO!' said the angry, weeping maid,
  'The charm is broken!—once betray'd,
  Never can this wrong'd heart rely
  On word or look, on oath or sigh.
Take back the gifts so fondly given,
With promis'd faith, and vows to heaven;
That little ring which night and morn,
With wedded truth my hand hath worn;
That seal which oft, in moments blest,
Thou hast upon my lips imprest,
And sworn its sacred spring should be
A fountain seal'd for only thee:
Take, take them back, the gift, the vow,
All sullied, lost, and hateful now!'

  I took the ring—the seal I took,
While, oh! her every tear and look
Were such as angels look and shed,
When man is by the world misled.
Gently I whisper'd, 'Fanny, dear!
Not half thy lover's gifts are here,
Say, where are all the kisses given,
From morn to noon, from noon to even,—
Those signets of true love, worth more
Than Solomon's own seal of yore—
Where are those gifts, so sweet, so many?
Come, dearest,—give back all, if any.'

While thus I whisper'd, trembling too
Lest all the nymph had sworn was true,
I saw a smile relenting rise
'Mid the moist azure of her eyes,
Like daylight o'er a sea of blue,
While yet in mid-air hangs the dew.
She let her cheek repose on mine,
She let my arm around her twine—
One kiss was half allowed, and then—
The ring and seal were her's again."

" SHE felt my lips' impassion'd touch—
'Twas the first time I dared so much.
And yet she chid not;
But whisper'd o'er my burning brow,
'Oh! do you doubt I love you now?'
Sweet soul! I did not."

"The Contract.

ECEIVE, dear maid, the warmest sigh
   That ever burst from lover's heart,
And let the beaming, tearful eye,
   What lips dare not reveal, impart

And, oh, return one look of love—
   One sigh of soft impassioned bliss,
Say but the impulse you approve,
   And seal the contract with a kiss."

"What do the ladies with their looks,
   Their kisses, and their smiles?
Can no receipts in those fair books
   Repair their former spoils?"

"False!

WITH a kiss my vow was greeted,
   As I knelt before thy shrine;
But I saw that kiss repeated
   On another lip than mine;
And a solemn vow was spoken
   That thy heart should not be changed;
But that binding vow was broken,
   And thy spirit was estranged!"

"I HAVE made a part of mine
All my lov'd one's being;
Trifling when he trifles,
Smiling when he smiles,
Mourning when he mourns,
And joyous when he joys;—
But when he, forgetting me,
Frequent kiss to other gives
O! I weep, I weep!"

"Come in the evening, or come in the morning;
Come when you're look'd for, or come without warning;
Kisses and welcome you'll find here before you,
And the oft'ner you come, the more I'll adore you."

"THY very look is life to me,
Thy smile like the clear moon rising,
And thy kiss is as sweet as the honey'd bee,
And more and more enticing."

"My gentle love, caressing and caress'd,
With heaving heart shall cradle me to rest,
Shed the warm tear-drop from her smiling eyes,
Lull with fond care, and med'cine me with sighs,
While finely flushing float her kisses meek,
Like melted rubies o'er my pallid cheek."

"She Kissed the Dead."

SHE kissed the dead. Her warm, red lips
    Were pressed against his marble brow,
'For if he's but asleep,' she said,
'And is not numbered with the dead,
    He'll rise and kiss me now.'

She kissed the dead. Her warm, red lips
    Were pressed against his hueless cheek,
'For he will know,' she softly said,
'My kiss; and if he be not dead,
    He'll turn to me and speak.'

She kissed the dead. Her warm, red lips
    Were pressed against his lips of ice.
'He answers not,' she weeping said;
'I know my darling must be dead,
    For I have kissed him thrice.'"

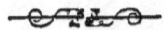

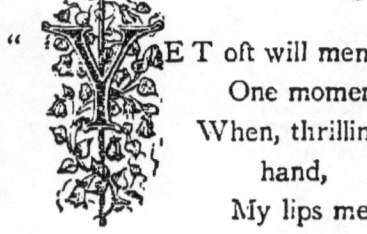

"YET oft will memory paint one happy scene,
    One moment fraught with ecstacy of bliss
When, thrilling with the soft clasp of thy hand,   [kiss;
    My lips meet thine in one long glowing
Ah, fatal gift! that was our parting doom—
How wert thou shadowed by fate's stern decree?
Alas! that clouds of sadness should have dimmed
    The first, the only boon of love from thee!"

"From yon island gentle breezes
  Waft a fragrance o'er the deep,
The kisses of a thousand flowers,
  Stolen from them while they sleep."

"Might we but share one wild caress,
  Ere life's autumnal blossoms fall,
And earth's brown, clinging lips impress
  The long cold kiss that waits us all."

"Kiss her gently, but be sly,
  Kiss her when there's no one by,
Steal your kiss, for then 'tis meetest—
  Stolen kisses are the sweetest!"

"The days, the weeks, the months of bliss
    That we, my love, have passed together,
Th' impression of your balmy kiss
    At Richmond, in the summer weather,

Shall long remain fixed in my mind,
    To please me when my spirit's low,
For they still leave a joy behind,
    To soften every sting of woe."

"Haply, when lock'd in sleep's embrace,
    Again I shall behold my Laura's face,—
      Again with transport hear
    Her voice soft whispering in my ear;
May steal once more a balmy kiss,
And taste, at least, of visionary bliss."

"Those ruby lips, where roses bloom
 And violets scatter sweet perfume;
 There, while entranc'd with rapt'rous joy,
 I snatch delicious kisses."

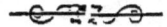

THE KISSES
OF
JOHANNES SECUNDUS.

Kiss I.
The Origin of the Kiss.

"WHEN in her lap the parent queen of love
Had borne Ascanius to Cythera's grove
On a sweet couch of tender violets made,
Hush'd in repose, her precious charge she laid,
Then all around bade milk-white roses bloom,
And every air impregn'd with sweet perfume.

Adonis' image to her mind return'd:
Once more her soul with tender passions burn'd;
And oft she cried, in ecstacy of joy
'Such was Adonis! such the lovely boy!'

Oft, as in rapture o'er the youth she hung,
Her eager arms around his neck had flung,
But fear'd to break the artless sleeper's rest,
And the fond ardour of her soul repress'd ;
And on each rose that blossom'd round his head
A thousand, thousand burning kisses shed ;
Beneath her lips the conscious flow'rets blush'd,
O'er every bud a warmer colour rush'd ;
While sighs in gently murmur'd sounds, confess'd
Each tender wish that struggled in her breast,
Where touch her lips the bursting buds disclose
A glowing kiss in every blushing rose,
And in each fresh-blown flow'ret multiply
The thrilling transports of Dione's joy.

But when again her native realm she sought,
Drawn by her cygnets o'er the azure vault,
As through the void her chariot roll'd along,
Thrice mutt'ring, as she went, the magic song ;
Like Celeus' son of old, her lavish hand
Shed kisses round, and fertiliz'd the land :
Thence for mankind the teeming harvest rose,
And hence the balm that mitigates my woes.

All hail ! ye kisses of ambrosial birth,
Whom rapture's thrilling hour produc'd on earth,
Sweet joys, that soothe the pangs of fierce desire,
For you the bard shall wake the sounding lyre ;
And while the Muses' hill shall last, your praise
Shall live immortal in the poet's lays ;

And love, who boasts himself, with conscious pride,
To that dear race from which ye spring allied,
In Roman strains your raptures shall rehearse
In all the liquid melody of verse."

KISS II.

"To crown our raptures 'twas agreed, dear maid,
    A sweet two thousand should the number be;
And on thy glowing lips a thousand paid,
    A thousand kisses I received of thee.
Complete, I own, the number'd raptures prove,
    But when did numbers e'er suffice with love?

When the ripe autumn yellows all the plain,
    Or spring with verdure clothes the blooming field
For number'd harvests ask the anxious swain,
    Or counts the blades the grassy meadows yield;
Or importunes with prayer the god of wine,
With number'd clusters to enrich the vine?

Who from the guardian of the hive demands
    A thousand honey-bees, yet asks no more?
Or when the Thunderer bids his lavish hands
    On the parch'd earth refreshing waters pour,
Strive we to count each drop of falling rain,
As the swift torrents moisten all the plain!

When Jove in terror clothes his angry arm,
    And hail descends, and wasting whirlwinds fly,
While earth and ocean, shook with pale alarm,
    Feel all the loosen'd vengeance of the sky,
Unmov'd he views the mischiefs they perform
Nor measures out the horrors of the storm.

Or good or ill alike descend from heaven,
    Extremes in both befit the race of Jove.
O thou! to whom celestial charms are given,
    Ah! why thus sparing of thy bounty prove?
O goddess! than that goddess lovelier far
Who roams blue oceans in her pearly car—

Why count thy kisses, and not count my sighs?
    Why count each kiss, nor count my every tear.
Those tears, that ever streaming from my eyes,
    Adown my cheeks and breast a channel wear?
Or cease to count thy kisses, or count all
The sighs that heave—the tears that streaming fall.

Yes, count my tears. Yet if thou cease to count,
    O cruel maid! each kiss thy lips bestow,

Then of my sorrows heed not the amount;
    But, oh! if such can mitigate my woe,
Let the unnumber'd tears these eyes have shed,
    By thy unnumber'd kisses be repaid."

Kiss III.

"Oh! brighter than that planet far,
    That sheds her silvery beams at eve,
Fairer than Venus' golden star,
    Sweet maid, a hundred balmy kisses give;
As many as th' impassion'd bard could crave,
As many as his beauteous Lesbia gave;

    As countless as the charms that play
        Around those lips with crimson dyed;
    As countless as the loves that stray
        O'er those fair cheeks, and in their blushes hide;
As countless as the lives your eyes impart;
As countless as the deaths your glances dart.

    As countless as the hopes and fears,
        As countless as the lover's sighs;
    As countless as the ceaseless cares
        That ever mingle with his tenderest joys,
Or as those arrows sheath'd within my breast,
Or those that still in love's bright quiver rest.

    But mingle all your balmy kisses
        With fond endearments, mirth and smiles;
    With soft delights, with murmuring blisses,
        With love-inspiring jests and wanton wiles;

So, in returning spring, the billing doves,
With quivering pinions interchange their loves.

   And while upon my cheek you lie,
      Your senses lost in amorous trance,
   And here and there in rapturous joy,
      Your passion-beaming eyes' voluptuous glance,
To me in sweetly plaintive murmurs sigh,
' Support me, dearest, for I faint, I die !'

   My circling arms around you throwing,
      I'll press you to my beating heart;
   And the long, humid kiss bestowing,
      Recall the fleeting sense, and life impart;
Till, with the frequent rapture breathless grown,
In dewy kisses I expire my own,

   And cry in accents faint and low,
      ' In those dear arms, my love, uphold me !'
   Then round me your fond arms you'll throw,
      And closely to your fostering bosom fold me;
And pressing on my lips the glowing kiss,
Call back my fainting soul to life, and bliss.

   Thus, lovely maid, while yet we may
      Improve the moments as they fly,
   While life is in its vernal day,
      And youth invites us with a smiling eye;
Soon with its cares will frowning age be here,
And pale disease, and death close pressing on his rear."

Kiss IV.

"A hundred sweet kisses by hundreds told o'er,
    I'll give those red lips, my dear charmer, of thine,
And thousands by thousands as lavishly pour
    On those cheeks, and those eyes that bewitchingly
        shine;
Till the sums of my raptures as numberless grow
    As the props that in ocean incessantly roll;
Or countless as those little orbits that glow
    In the mantle of night when it covers the pole.

But, oh! when entranc'd on thy bosom I lie,
    And my lips to thy lips with fond ardour adhere;
When I kiss thy fair cheeks or thy tale-telling eye,
    The charms that I gaz'd on at once disappear.
The sweet pouting lips that inspir'd with delight,
    The beam of those eyes that bewitch'd me the while;
The rose on thy cheeks—are all snatch'd from my sight,
    And the dimple that laughs in thy delicate smile.

That delicate smile that, with solacing beam,
    Dispels from my soul all the darkness of woe,
And enlivening my bosom with Hope's cheering gleam,
    Bids the sigh cease to heave, and the tear-drop to
        flow.
So Sol when he rises, dispels from the sky
    The mists that would gather, and darken his way,
And borne on his gem-studded chariot on high,
    From the cloudless serene pours the splendour of day.

Ah, me! thus, by jealous emotion possess'd
    What rivalry glows 'twixt my lips and my eyes!
Each fondly admires thee, and longs to be blest,
    And envies the pleasure the other enjoys.

Then, oh! if with jealousy eyes disagree,
    Nor my lips bear a rival in rapture, my love,
Can I bear that another should emulate me,
    And share in thy smiles, though that rival be Jove?"

Kiss V.

" 'Gainst thee, my life, he stood prepar'd to wing
The fiery shaft, and stretch'd the sounding string;
But when thy blooming cheeks, thy forehead fair,
The wanton ringlets of thy flowing hair,
And those thy gently heaving breasts he spied,
Those breasts that with his beauteous mother's vied,
Love paus'd in doubt, enamour'd of thy charms,
Then flung the dart aside, and sought thy arms;
There on thy lips with childish transport hung,
And kiss'd and wanton'd as he fondly clung—
Breath'd Cyprian odours in each kiss he press'd,
And fill'd with fragrant sweets thy inmost breast,
Then by each god the solemn oath he swore,
And lovely Venus, ne'er to harm thee more,
What wonder then such sweets thy kiss imbue
Such balmy fragrance, such ambrosial dew!
What wonder then thy heart can never prove,
Oh, cruel maid! the gentle fires of love!"

Kiss VI.

"Not certain kisses please my changeful mind,
Each has its varied rapture undefin'd;
So, when thy humid lips encounter mine,
Sweet is the humid kiss which flows from thine;
So ardent kisses ardent joys impart,
And the warm transport thrills within the heart;
So when thine eyes with tender passion glow,
'Tis sweet to kiss the authors of my woe;
'Tis sweet to kiss thy cheeks, and breathless lie
On thy fair neck with rapturous ecstacy,
And on thy rosy cheeks the joy indite,
Thy shoulders fair, and bosom snowy white;
And while our glowing lips, in amorous play,
In rapture meet and snatch the kiss away,
'Tis bliss to feel, as lips with lips unite,
Our souls commingling with the dear delight—
The heart forsaking with the fleeting breath—
While love lies panting on the brink of death.

To me, or whether to thy lips I give,
Or from thy ruby lips the kiss receive,
Or the long kiss, when lips to lips adhere,
The soft, the rapid,—all alike are dear,
Only be thine, with sweet ingenious art,
Each kiss to vary that thy lips impart:
Nor what thy lips receive on mine bestow,
So shall our joys with varied transports flow!
But let the first who from this pact shall swerve
With meek submissive looks this law observe!

'As many kisses each at first may give,
As many kisses each at first receive,
So many kisses shall the vanquish'd pay,
So many kisses varied every way.'"

Kiss VII.

"A brighter crimson, with the morning light,
　Blushes the rose impearl'd with nightly dew,
　So glow thy ruby lips with brighter hue,
Moist with the kisses of a rapturous night;
　And thy fair cheeks a fairer tint assume
From violets, as some hand of lily white;
　So new ripe cherries shine 'midst lingering bloom,
When spring and summer in the tree unite.
　But, ah! when thus thy kisses sweetest flow,
Why forc'd to leave thee, and forego their charms!
　Still let thy lips retain that beauteous glow
Till eve restores me to thy circling arms!"

Kiss VIII.

"Oh, cease the balmy kiss, and cease awhile
The murmur'd rapture, the endearing smile;
Nor always thus your arms around me twine,
And faint, and breathless on my neck recline;

E'en pleasure has its bounds; the rapturous joy
Repeated oft, will lose its zest, and cloy.
When thrice three kisses from thy lips I sue,
Withhold the seven, and give me only two;
Nor these with too much rapture be replete,
Nor yet too long, nor yet too balmy sweet;
Such as chaste Dian' to her brother gives,
Or from some artless maid her sire receives;
Then bursting from my arms, with bounding feet,
Fly swift, and hide you in some dark retreat;
Close I'll pursue through each perplexing shade,
Search every spot, and find where you are laid,

And, as the towering falcon bears away
The timid dove, I'll seize my beauteous prey.
Around me then your suppliant arms you'll fling,
And hang upon my neck, and closely cling,
And on my lips seven coaxing kisses press,
And with endearments sue for your release,
But sue in vain: not seven shall set you free,
But seven times seven the price of freedom be;
Still shall my glowing arms your neck enfold,
And captive still my beauteous wanton hold.
Then, when you pay the balmy ransom, swear
By all your graces, all your charms, my fair,
That oft again such frolics you'll pursue
And oft for faults like these such balmy sums be due."

Kiss IX.

"Faint with the rapturous joy, and breathless grown,
Around thy neck my languid arms were thrown,
And on thy burning lips, prepar'd to part,
Hover'd my soul, and ceas'd to warm my heart;
Pale Styx already swam before my sight,
And hell's grim pilot, and the shades of night,
When, gently breathing from thy inmost breast
Thy lips on mine a humid kiss impress'd!
That kiss redeem'd me from the Stygian vale
And bade the infernal vessel freightless sail,
But, ah! no freightless voyage the pilot made.
Still in these regions flits my plaintive shade;

Breath'd in this frame, a part of thee remains,
Part of thy soul, and these faint limbs sustain;
But through each passage, eager to be free,
It pants, it struggles, to revert to thee;
And, oh! unless thy fostering breath retain,
Life will desert this sinking frame again.
Then to my lips thy lips, Neæra, join
And with thy soul sustain this soul of mine!
So, when this scene of life and love is o'er,
From our joint frames one single soul shall soar."

Kiss X.

"Why tempt me with those lips of scarlet glow?
For learn, O maiden, with the flinty breast,

Ne'er shall those proffer'd lips by mine be press'd!
Since you would have me prize your kisses so,
Those cold, cold kisses, whence no raptures flow,

That when, all glowing with the wild desire,
  In every pulse I feel the scorching fire,
As the warm life-blood rushes to and fro;
You thus refuse me, and my pangs deride.
  But whither now? Oh! fly me not, but stay;
Oh! turn not, turn not those sweet lips aside;
  Oh! turn not thus those sparkling eyes away;
Yes! I will kiss thee, to thy lips be press'd,
Dear maid, more gentle far than cygnet's downy breast!"

Kiss XI.

"Give me, sweet maid, one little kiss,
  One little kiss, I said, and sigh'd,
Scarce had I felt the thrilling bliss,
  Scarce were your glowing lips to mine applied,

When from my lips your lips you take
  In sudden haste, and burst away;

So, when he feels the coiling snake,
    The heedless rustic startles in dismay.

Not this to give the balmy kiss!
    Ah! no, my love, but in the mind
To raise the fond idea of bliss
    Then leave the sting of fierce desire behind."

Kiss XII.

" 'Tis not a kiss those ruby lips bestow,
    But richest nectar, and ambrosial dews;
Such as from fragrant nard or cassia flow;
    Or blest Arabia's spicy shrubs diffuse;
Or sweets, that from Hymettus' thymy brow,
    Or roses that Cecropian bowers produce,
Unwearied honey-bees selecting bear
To cells of virgin wax, and temper there.
    But if thy vermeil lips, in ev'ry kiss,
Thus give to banquet on celestial fare,
    And thrill my soul with ecstacy of bliss,
Soon shall this frame imbibe celestial powers,
And I shall revel in Olympian bowers.
Then shall thy precious boon, Neæra, spare,
Or with me those immortal honours share!
For ev'n should Jove, by rebel godheads driven,
To me resign the majesty of heaven—
That heaven, without thy presence, were unblest,
And all is nectar'd feasts without a zest!"

Kiss XIII.

"While circled by those fond, endearing arms,
    That here and there in amorous fervour twine,
Neæra, you, with soul-entrancing charms,
    Or on my neck, or shoulder soft recline,
And, fondly hanging o'er, unfold to sight
That beauteous neck, and bosom snowy white;
    And to my lips your glowing lips you join,
And on my cheek the thrilling joy indite,
Then, gently murmuring, chide your ardent swain,
    If the fond jest he pay you back again.

While to my lips, in tremulous ecstacy,
    Your lips, dear maid, the thrilling kiss impart;
And, breathing forth the sweetly murmur'd sigh,
    Pour your warm spirit through my raptur'd heart—
That sigh to me with genial life replete
So softly musical, so balmy sweet;
    While you, Neæra, snatch my breath away,
That, glowing with my bosom's inward heat,
    Fleets on my lips, and 'most forgets to play;

And, O! sweet soother of my passion's rage!
    Once more, with that re-animating breath,
Recall my spirit from the gates of death,
    And the fierce ardour of my soul assuage;
Impassion'd with the bliss—'With Love,' I cry,
'O'er every power supreme in sovereignty—

With Love, nor god nor mortal can compare;
But, oh! with him if any power can vie,
  'Tis you, Neæra, you, my charming fair!'"

The Repulse.

"ONE kiss you earnestly implore,
  And I, for this, dear youth, must fly thee:
That boon obtain'd, you'd ask for more,
  And I, alas! could not deny thee.

For short would be love's tender tie,
  That strives to bind thy heart in vain;
And then the hapless maid might sigh,
  While thou wouldst triumph in her pain."

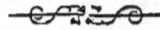

THE KISSES

OF

JEAN BONNEFONS.

Kiss I.

"NYMPH, all other nymphs excelling,
    On whose lips, so rosy bright,
All my hopes of bliss are dwelling,
    Source of every fond delight.

Gentle nymph, on whom is lavish'd
    Ev'ry sweet, enchanting grace,
Charms from other beauties ravish'd,
    To adorn thy lovely face.

While my heart, with passion glowing,
    Calls thee loveliest, dearest, best,
Wilt thou, the soft kiss bestowing,
    Soothe its pains, and give it rest?

No, ah no! withhold the blessing,
    Keep the dang'rous boon away;
Let its thrilling touch, increasing,
    Bid the flame more fiercely prey;

But thy lips to mine applying,
    Gently steal my breath away;

Till with rapture fainting, dying,
    Ev'ry pulse forgets to play.

No, ah, no! ev'n that were danger,
    And my soul might wing her flight,
And be, dearest girl, a ranger
    In those realms of endless night.

Where, condemn'd to gloom and sadness,
    Plaintive spirits ever stray;
Where love ne'er cheers, nor mirth, nor
    E'er beguile the ling'ring day.   [gladness,

Yet come! to mine thy lips applying,
    Steal me from myself away;

Till with rapture fainting, dying,
  My soul, loos'd from these bonds of clay,

Hovers where in dark meanders
  Styx rolls on his lurid tide;
Where the soft Catullus wanders
  With Tibullus by his side.

I, too, in turn, my lips applying,
  Will gently steal thy honied breath,
Till thy soul enraptur'd, flying,
  Hastens to the realms beneath;

And in those bright regions hovers,
  Where so sweetly, side by side,
Undivided from their lovers,
  Nemesis and Lesbia glide.

For within that realm of spirits
  Tend'rest joys await the bless'd;
Each his former love inherits—
  Still possessing, still possess'd.

There, my lovely girl, I'll meet thee,
  Pale and trembling, on that coast;
And with rapturous kisses greet thee,
  Till in silent wonder lost—

E'en those bards, whose gentle measures,
  Told of bliss, and taught the way;
Who, o'er love's delightful pleasures,
  Held the undisputed sway.

All, with one accord, shall hail us
    Welcome to the blissful grove,
And confess that none excel us
    In the tender arts of love."

Kiss II.

"Clasp'd, sweet maid, in thy embrace,
While I view thy smiling face,
And the sweets with rapture sip,
Flowing from thy honied lip;
Then I taste in heav'nly state
All that's happy, all that's great.

But when you forsake my arms,
And displeasure clouds thy charms,
Sudden, I, who proved so late
All that's happy, all that's great—
Prove the tortures of a ghost
Wandering on the Stygian coast."

Kiss III.

Fairest of blossoms, on whose lips the rose
    Hath left its sweetness; from the wanton wreaths
Of whose bright ringlets and whose bosom flows
    Fragrance like that the vernal violet breathes,
Or the od'rous shrubs of Araby exhale,
Flinging their spicy sweets on ev'ry passing gale:

Come, breathe, then, from thy lips, and gently press
   On mine the honied dews of many a kiss,
   Rapt'rous and warm with love, and numberless,
   Like young doves be our interchange of bliss,
And, not like her, the Roman maid of old,
Who counted the sweet store—oh! be not thou so cold.

Come, dearest, with thy smiling lips apart,
   Pouring a show'r of kisses sweet, then join
Them closer still, and from thy inmost heart
   Breathe forth thy soul, and let it mix with mine:
But mingle, so that never art shall sever,
And like our endless love be thus conjoined for ever."

Kiss IV.

"I mourn not that the soft melodious tone
   Of thy sweet voice hath, like enchantment, reft
   My ev'ry sense, or that my soul has left
This feeble clay untenanted, and flown,
To join in pleasing dalliance with thine own,
   Lur'd from me by thy moist lips, when I quaff'd
   Of dewy kisses the ambrosial draught;
Nor that my foolish heart from me hath gone
To dwell with thee; ah! no, I only sigh
   To think that when, with fast-receding breath,
In the delirious trance of ecstacy.
   My spirit hovers on the brink of death,

'Twill not at that dear moment wholly fly,
And let me in thy fond embraces sweetly die."

Kiss V.

" And wouldst thou have me hide the smart
    That thrills in every aching vein;
And with dissimulative art,
    Conceal from all my inward pain?

Thou know'st not what the task would be:
    Did fires like these within thee prey,
No, not all thy philosophy
    Could charm the urchin, Love, away.

Can I behold each auburn tress
    That wantons round her lovely neck,
Lips that were surely made to bless,
    And th' rose that blooms on either cheek,

Nor deem e'en kingdoms cheaply lost
    For one short hour of rapt'rous bliss,
Give all that ever Ind' can boast
    To snatch one dear delicious kiss?

Perish the wretch that could behold
    Beauties like these with careless eye;
To all love's warmer raptures cold,
    Unheeded let him live and die."

Kiss VI.
To a Lap Dog.

"Bless'd is thy lot, supremely bless'd;
　　Who sees must envy thee;
Thus by that gentle hand caress'd,
And fondled in the rosy breast
　　Of that fair queen of chastity.

Diverted by thy artless play,
　　Companion of her home,
With thee she sports the live-long day,
And makes thee partner of her way,
　　When fancy leads her steps to roam.

Her daily meal she bids thee share,
　　And, with unfeign'd delight,
Selecting with attentive care,
The choicest morsels for thy fare,
　　Provokes thy little appetite.

Then when the sweet repast is o'er,
    Strives with new joys to bless;
Takes to her fragrant breast once more
And kisses sweet, a balmy store,
    Her lips more prodigally press,

Than he, of such delights the sire,
    From Lesbia crav'd of old;
Catullus, whose sweet sounding lyre
Breath'd the soft notes of fond desire,
    And all love's tender raptures told.

Bless'd is thy lot, supremely bless'd,
    With all love's sweetest store!
And is there whose insatiate breast
With soft delights like thee possess'd,
    Would madly wish, and sigh for more?

And yet there is, by thee enjoy'd,
    E'en gods would give, to share,
The spangl'd heaven in which they pride,
Like thee to slumber by her side
    All the night long, and wanton there.

Sweet fav'rite, while 'tis thine to share
    What all with envy see;
For this her kindness, this her care
Let gratitude reward the fair
    With pleasing, fond fidelity."

Kiss VII.

"Let me kiss those soft lids, my dear joy,
  Where those glances bewitchingly play
Let me kiss those bright tresses that vie
  With the god who illumines the day.

Ah! wouldst thou, ungrateful, deny
  To the poet so slight a request?
No, no, I can read in thine eye
  The denial was only in jest.

Thou wouldst be but provokingly coy,
  And seem to deny it to me;
With refusal enhance the sweet joy,
  And tempt me to snatch it from thee.

Then thus in my arms will I fold thee,
  Thus circle that white neck of thine;
Thus—thus to my bosom I'll hold thee,
  And thus press those moist lips to mine.

Thou mayst pout, and look gloomy, and threat me
    And struggle to guard our own bliss;
With scratches and pinches beset me,
    While I snatch away kiss after kiss.

I'll fear not the threats thou mayst make,
    And laugh at each fruitless endeavour:
In my arms thee more firmly I'll take,
    And kiss thee still closer than ever.

Oh! dearer to me are the joys
    That spring from sweet struggles like these,
For we deem it no longer a prize
    If we can enjoy when we please.

Then, oh! wouldst thou heighten the bliss?
    Thus ever, my Pancharis, fly me;
Thus, thus, let me snatch the sweet kiss
    Thus ever resist, and deny me."

Kiss VIII.

"Silly thing, in search of bliss,
    Didst thou dare to touch her lip,
And in each delicious kiss,
    Balmy dews of nectar sip?

Tempt the sweet repast no more
    For in every kiss's breath,
While thou sipp'st the honied store,
    Deadly poison lurks beneath.

Though the liquid ardours flow
    Swiftly through each vital part,

Till in ev'ry pulse they glow,
    And consume thy aching heart.

Still unmindful of the past,
    To her ruby lips thou fliest,
And there madly dar'st to taste
    The honied bliss by which thou diest.

In those lips of rosy hue
    .Pain and pleasure mingled lie;
Oh! how sweetly they undo,
    By how many arts destroy!

Fair destroyers of my peace,
    Why so many pangs impart?
Cease those fiery torments, cease,
    And no more distract my heart.

Give me sweets, but give them pure;
    When I seek the balmy kiss;
Let me sip, but sip secure,
    Nor with tortures taint the bliss."

Kiss IX.

"Then hear me, goddess, thou, whose care benign,
    Guards watchful o'er the lover's destiny,
    If, when again in am'rous ecstasy
On her fair bosom breathless I recline,
Life should forsake this feeble frame of mine,
    And my frail spirit bursts her bonds of clay;
    For such may yet arrive, when slow decay

Hath weaken'd every barrier; be it thine,
Sweet pow'r, to guide the disembodied sprite
　　To thy fair mansions, where for ever reign,
In sunny regions of celestial light,
　　Laughter, and mirth, and joy, unmixed with pain;
There, in the green recesses of the bless'd,
Lulled in Elysian raptures, let me rest."

Kiss X.

"While round thee my fond arms I twine,
And press my glowing lips to thine,

And eager of the bliss, inhale
The balmy breath's nectareous gale.
Lost in the ecstacies of love,
I seem to soar in worlds above,

And seem, my fair one, seem to be
E'en happier than divinity."

Kiss XI.

"How can two such extremes combine,
    Dear maid, in thee;
That, when such sweetness all is thine,
    Sweeter than sweet can be,
Thy lips such bitterness impart
And from thine eyes envenom'd sorrows dart?

    But when thou art so bitter all,
        To such degree,
    That all the bitterness of gall
        Cannot e'en equal thee:
Why are thy kisses then so sweet,
And with ambrosial dews thy lips replete?

    Why do the glances of thine eyes
        No longer sting,
    But with each shaft that with them flies
        Such gentle pleasures bring?
Is't in thy lips, I pr'ythee tell,
Or in thy glances that such virtues dwell;

    That thus at times my soul they bless
        With bitter joy,
    And now with honied bitterness
        Oppress me and destroy?
    Oh! bitterness too cloying sweet:
Oh! sweet with too much bitterness replete?"

Kiss XII.

"Give me, sweet life, the kiss that's ripe
    With honied moisture sweet,
That will assuage the fires that rage
    With such consuming heat:

And with the dew that doth imbue
    Thy lips, so ruby bright,
Bid them allay the flames that play
    Within me day and night.

Oh! no, forbear, my gentle fair,
    I know not what I sue;
Oh! keep away from me, I pray,
    Those lips that might undo,

And fan the fire of fierce desire,
    Till, glowing in my heart,
O'er all my soul the torrents roll,
    Consuming ev'ry part.

Why snatch from me so hastily
    The lip that presses mine?
Oh! come and pour the burning shower
    Of kisses all from thine.

Let me expire by their sweet fire,
    Till, from each burning kiss,
Like him I rise, who, to the skies,
    From Œta soar'd to bliss."

Horace.

" CRUEL who hurts the fragrant kiss
   Which Venus bathes with quintessence of
      bliss."

" While now her bending neck she plies
   Backward to meet the burning kiss,
   Then with an easy cruelty denies,
   Yet wishes you would snatch, not ask the bliss."

" 'Twas night, and heav'n, intent with all its eyes,
      Gaz'd on the deceitful maid :
      A thousand pretty things she said,
      A thousand kisses sweetly paid
   From me, deluded me, her falsehood to disguise.

She clasp'd me in her soft encircling arms,
    She press'd her glowing cheeks to mine,
    The clinging ivy, or the curling vine,
    Did never yet so closely twine ;
Who could be man and bear the lustre of her charms?

And thus she swore—'By all the powers above,
    When winter storms shall cease to roar,
    When summer suns shall shine no more
    When wolves their cruelty give o'er,
Neæra then, and not till then, shall cease to love.'

Ah! false Neæra! perjured fair! but know,
    I have a soul too great to bear
    A rival's proud insulting air ;
    Another may be found as fair,
As fair, ungrateful nymph ! and far more just than thou.

Shouldst thou repent, and at my feet be laid,
    Dejected, penitent, forlorn,
    And all thy former follies mourn,
    Thy proffer'd passion I would scorn ;
The gods shall do me right on that devoted head."

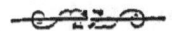

Cannazar.

"OH! give, when I ask thee, as many fair kisses
    As fair Lesbia gave to her poet of yore;
'Till not e'en the stars shall outnumber our blisses,
    Or sands that are spread on the surge-beaten shore.

Let their sums be as countless as leaves that are playing
    On the forest's green boughs when the summer is near,
Or the hues of the field when, with flow'rets arraying
    Its bosom, spring breathes her warm gale on the year;

Or the fishes that swim in the ocean's deep bosom,
    Or pinions that beat the wide vault in their flight;
Or the bees that, still roving, from blossom to blossom,
    Collect their sweet treasures by morn's early light.

If these, my dear maid, by thy bounty be given,
    As countless and sweet as thy lover demands,
For them would he spurn all the raptures of heaven,
    And the nectar that sparkles in Ganymede's hands.'

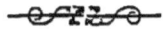

Ovid.

"SMILING, she said—'How grateful thy request,
If e'er my kisses please thee, take the best.'
Oh! with what gust, as from her soul they came,
Such might melt Jove, and stop the vengeful flame!"

"With what a gust, ye gods, we then embrac'd,
How every kiss was dearer than the last."

"They all appear to shun the bliss,
But when they once have felt a kiss,
They long and sigh for others."

"Nor fret I thou in kissing shouldst excel,
And yet, 'tis strange to know to kiss so well."

The Story of Narcissus.

"THERE stands a fountain in a darksome wood,
   Nor stain'd with falling leaves nor rising
      mud;
   Untroubled by the breath of winds it rests
   Unsully'd by the touch of men or beasts;
High bow'rs of shady trees above it grow,
And rising grass and cheerful greens below.
Pleas'd with the form and coolness of the place
And over-heated by the morning chase
Narcissus on the grassy verdure lies:

And as his own bright image he survey'd,
He fell in love with the fantastic shade;

And o'er the fair resemblance hung unmov'd,
Nor knew, fond youth! it was himself he lov'd.
The well-turn'd neck and shoulders he descries,
The spacious forehead, and the sparkling eyes;
The hands that Bacchus might not scorn to show,
And hair that round Apollo's head might flow;
With all the purple youthfulness of face,
That gently blushes in the wat'ry glass.
By his own flames consum'd the lover lies,
And gives himself the wound by which he dies.
To the cold water oft he joins his lips,
Oft catching at the beauteous shade he dips
His arms, as often from himself he slips.
Nor knows he who it is his arms pursue
With eager clasps, but loves he knows not who.

What could, fond youth, this helpless passion move?
What kindled in thee this unpity'd love?
Thy own warm blush within the water glows
With thee the colour'd shadow comes and goes,
Its empty being on thyself relies;
Step thou aside, and the frail charmer dies.

Still o'er the fountain's wat'ry gleam he stood,
Mindless of sleep, and negligent of food;
Still view'd his face, and languish'd as he view'd,
At length he rais'd his head, and thus began
To vent his griefs and tell the woods his pain—
'You trees,' says he, ' and thou surrounding grove,
Who oft have been the kindly scenes of love,

Tell me, if e'er within your shades did lie
A youth so tortur'd, so perplex'd as I?
I, who before me see the charming fair
Whilst there he stands, and yet he stands not there.
In such a maze of love my thoughts are lost;
And yet no bulwark'd town, nor distant coast,
Preserves the beauteous youth from being seen,
No mountains rise, nor oceans flow between,
A shallow water hinders my embrace;
And yet the lovely mimic wears a face
That kindly smiles, and when I bend to join
My lips to his, he fondly bends to mine,
Hear, gentle youth, and pity my complaint,
Come from thy well, thou fair inhabitant.
My charms an easy conquest have obtained
O'er other hearts, by thee alone disdain'd.
But why should I despair? I'm sure he burns
With equal flames, and languishes by turns.
Whene'er I stoop, he offers at a kiss,
And when my arms I stretch, he stretches his.
His eye with pleasure on my face he keeps,
He smiles my smiles, and when I weep he weeps.
Whene'er I speak, his moving lips appear
To utter something which I cannot hear.

 Ah wretched me! I now begin too late
To find out all the long perplex'd deceit;
It is myself I love, but self I see;
The gay delusion is a part of me

I kindle up the fires by which I burn
And my own beauties from the well return.
How gladly would I from myself remove!
And at a distance set the thing I love.
And now I faint with grief; my fate draws nigh;
In all the pride of blooming youth I die.
Death will the sorrows of my heart relieve.
Oh, might the visionary youth survive,
I should with joy my latest breath resign!
But, oh! I see his fate involv'd in mine.'

This said, the weeping youth again return'd
To the clear fountain, where again he burn'd.
His tears defac'd the surface of the well

With circle after circle, as they fell;
And now the lovely face but half appears,
O'errun with wrinkles, and deform'd with tears.
'Ah, whither,' cries Narcissus, 'dost thou fly?
Let me still feed the flame by which I die;

Let me still see, tho' I'm no further blest.'
Then rends his garments off, and beats his breast
His naked bosom redden'd with the blow,
In such a blush as purple clusters show,
Ere yet the sun's autumnal heat refine
Their sprightly juice, and mellow'd it to wine.
The glowing beauties of his breast he spies,
And with a new redoubled passion dies.
As wax dissolves, as ice begins to run,
And trickle into drops before the sun;
So melts the youth, and languishes away,
His beauty withers, and his limbs decay;
And none of those attractive charms remain
To which the slighted echo su'd in vain."

"WINDS! whisper gently while she sleeps,
    And fan her with your cooling wings,
While she her drops of beauty weeps
    From pure and yet unrivall'd springs.

Glide over beauty's field, her face;
    To kiss her lip and cheek be bold:
But with a calm and stealing pace,
    Neither too rude, nor yet too cold.

Play in her beams and crisp her hair,
    With such a gale as wings soft love;

And with so sweet, so rich an air
    As breathes from the Arabian grove.

A breath as hush'd as lover's sigh,
    Or that unfolds the morning's door;
Sweet as the winds that gently fly
    To sweep the spring's enamell'd door."

" Like doves we would be billing,
    And clip and kiss so fast,
Yet he would be unwilling,
    That I should kiss the last."

" The billows kiss the shore, and then
Flow back into the deep again,
    As tho' they did not kiss."

"CONTENT to frame some new design of bliss,
    The wanton Cyprian queen composed a kiss.
    An ample portion of ambrosial juice
    With mystic skill she temper'd first for use.
    This done, her infant work was well bedew'd
With choicest nectar; and o'er all she strew'd
Part of the honey which shy Cupid stole,
Much to his cost, and blended with the whole;
Then that soft scent which from the violet flows
She mix'd with spoils of many a vernal rose;

Each gentle blandishment in love we find,
Each graceful winning gesture, next she join'd
And all those joys that in her zone abound,
Made up the kiss, and the rich labour crown'd.
Consid'ring now what beauteous nymph might prove
Worthy the gift, and worthy of her love,
She fixed on Chloe as her fav'rite maid,
To whom the goddess, sweetly smiling, said—
'Take this, my fair, to perfect every grace,
And on thy lips the fragrant blessing place.'"

"Our vicar he calls it damnation to sip
  The ripe ruddy dew of a woman's dear lip,
Says that Beelzebub lurks in her kerchief so sly,
  And Apollyon shoots darts from her merry black eye;
Yet, whoop, Jack! kiss Gillian the quicker,
Till she bloom like a rose—and a fig for the vicar!"

Muret.

"WHEN my fond lips would snatch the kiss,
My eyes with envy view the bliss, [dwell;
And fear to lose those charms on which they
And, oh! whene'er I strive to raise
My eyes to you, and fondly gaze,
At once my lips the vain attempt repel.
Such are the charms your lips display,
So tempt me with their rosy hue,
As steel the magnet's force, so they
At once attract my lips to you.
Thus, beauteous tyrant, you control, [soul."
Thus steal me from myself, and sway my am'rous

Fontanus.

"WHEN thy clos'd lips the joyless kiss impart,
Nor thy warm breath comes glowing from
thy heart,
A something saddens all my soul, I feel
E'en on my lips the silent kiss grow chill.
But when thy swelling lips reply to mine,
And my warm spirit flies to thine,
My pulses fail, sense, strength, and colour fly,
And pale and breathless in thine arms I lie.

Come, kiss me close, and with each glowing kiss,
O let our spirits mingle into bliss!
But leave no space through which my soul can fly,
Lest in thy circling arms thy lover die."

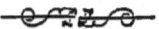

"GIVE me, Lydia, kisses sweet,
    Kisses, love's delicious treat;
    Honied kisses from thy lip,
    Cupid's self might joy to sip,
    Sweeter than the flowers which bloom,
And around shed rich perfume—
Softer than the zephyr's breath,
Wafted o'er the flowry heath!

Freely give thy soul to joy;
Mercenary pleasures cloy,
While the voluntary bliss,
Kiss so sweetly answering kiss,
Fills the soul with real pleasure,
Bless'd and blessing without measure."

"I wish that I were
    A voiceless sigh,
    Floating through air
    When thy beauty draws nigh:
Unperceived I would steal o'er thy cheek of down,
And kiss thy soft lip unchecked by a frown."

Gallus.

"MY goddess, Lydia; heav'nly fair,
As lilies sweet, as soft as air,
Let loose thy tresses, spread thy charms,
And to my love give fresh alarms.

Oh! let me gaze on those bright eyes,
Though sacred lightning from them flies;
Show me that soft, that modest grace,
Which paints with charming red thy face.

Give me ambrosia in a kiss,
That I may rival Jove in bliss;
That I may mix my soul with thine
And make the pleasure all divine."

"Oh! heavenly fool, thy most kiss-worthy face
Anger invests with such a lovely grace,
That anger's self I needs must kiss again."

Baif.

"COME hither, and give me moist kisses,
    Dear girl, such as none ever gave!
What! wouldst thou then number my blisses,
    And ask me how many I'll have!

I know not the number of kisses
    That Lesbia was ask'd for, or gave;
But sure, who can number his blisses
    Can never have many to crave."

Bonfadius.

"YE grots, ye groves, were witness of my bliss,
When from her lips I snatch'd the nectar'd kiss!
The thrilling joy of life, and sense bereft,
And on her humid lips my soul was left,
But when she saw me pale, and breathless laid,
With fond encircling arms the lovely maid
My languid form drew closer to her breast,
And on my lips a sweeter kiss impress'd;

And scarce had I inhal'd the balmy dew,
When to my heart my wand'ring spirit flew.
To me now dearer is the vital flame,
Since from her lips, her ruby lips, it came."

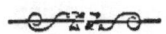

Buchanan.

"WITH ev'ry kiss those lips, my fair, bestow
Such nectar'd streams, such rich ambrosia flow,
With gods I seem their heav'nly state to share,
With gods I banquet on celestial fare;
And lost in pleasing dreams of ecstasy,
Seem far more bless'd than e'en a god can be.
But, oh! whene'er those balmy kisses flow,
With falsehood mix'd, and treach'ry lurks below,
Then instant I, who shar'd the realms of bliss,
Plunge headlong down to hell's profound abyss;
In darker horrors lost, and deeper woe
Than those that suffer in that world below!"

Anacreontic.

"FILL'D to thee, to thee I drank,
   I nothing did but drink and fill;
The bowl by turns was bright and blank
   'Twas drinking, filling, drinking still.

At length I bid an artist paint
   Thy image in this ample cup,

That I might see the dimpled saint,
   To whom I quaff'd my nectar up.

Behold how bright that purple lip
   Now blushes through the wave at me
And every roseate drop I sip
   Is just like kissing wine from thee.

And still I drink the more for this;
   For, ever when the draught I drain,
Thy lip invites another kiss,
   And in the nectar flows again.

So, here's to thee, my gentle dear,
   And may that eyelid never shine
Beneath a darker, bitterer tear
   Than bathes it in this bowl of mine."

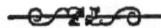

"THERE is a sweet, a pleasing death;
   A soft suspension of the breath,
      Replete with tenderest bliss:
I find it in my Lucy's arms,
I taste it in her ripen'd charms,
      And in her murm'ring kiss.
Wild fancy riots in the thought
Of rapture with endearment fraught
      What mortal sense like this?
For you to catch my fleeting breath,
To share in that delicious death
      Which hovers on your kiss."

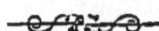

Sappho.

"HITHER, Venus! queen of kisses,
  This shall be the night of blisses:
  This the night, to friendship dear,
  Thou shalt be our Hebe here.
  Fill the golden brimmer high,
  Let it sparkle like thine eye;
  Bid the rosy current gush,
  Let it mantle like thy blush."

Guarini.

"WHEN o'er the virgin cheek we meet
    Health's tender blooming roses spread,
  To kiss those roses may be sweet,
    To kiss them on their native bed.

Full well experienc'd lovers know,
    And chief, the few who blissful burn,
  That kiss is lifeless we bestow
    On charms that yield no kind return,

Be sure those kisses breathe delight,
  Where love the sweetly vengeful dart
Exchanges, while fond lips unite,
  Lips echoing soft as kisses part.

When one warm wish inflames the pair,
  Not less endearing kisses prove;
Each gives, each takes, an equal share,
  Sweet interchange of sweetest love.

Kiss the dear lip the swelling breast,
  The snow-white hand, the forehead kiss!
'Tis by the lip the joy's expresse'd,
  'Tis the kind lip repays the bliss.

When lovers' lips in transport join,
  Their souls to share that transport fly;
And as their mingling breaths combine,
  The purple gems with life supply.

Then each inspired kiss imparts
  In sounds half utter'd, half suppressed,
The tender secrets of their hearts,
  Secrets to lips alone confess'd,

When soul is thus with soul entwined
  The living rapture is improved;
'Tis rapture of the sweetest kind
  To kiss when kissed, to love when loved."

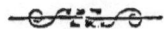

"SHE smil'd consenting, and her lips impart
  To my parch'd lips one dear delicious kiss,
Whose breath that instant to my fainting heart
  Recall'd my spirit from the dark abyss:
A humid kiss, rich with ambrosial dews,
And all the spicy sweets Arabia's shrubs diffuse."

"HE felt her flesh, (his fancy thought it such),
  And fear'd to hurt her with too rude a
      touch.
He kiss'd her with belief so strong and vain,
That he imagin'd how she kiss'd again."

Pasquier.

"DEAR maid, a gentle kiss impart,
   Like that in innocence of heart,
Which some young girl, with fond caresses,
   On her fair sister's cheek impresses;
For joys like that, so pure and chaste,
   Must ever please, and ever last."

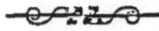

Plato.

"WHENE'ER thy nectar'd kiss I sip,
   And drink thy breath, in melting twine,
My soul then flutters to my lip,
   Ready to fly and mix with thine."

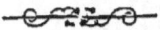

"See! the mountains kiss high heaven,
   And the waves clasp one another;
No sister flower would be forgiven
   If it disdained its brother:
And the sunlight clasps the earth,
   And the moonbeams kiss the sea—
What are all these kisses worth
   If thou kiss not me!"

"Why, Anna, why let sparrows sip
   The nectar from your rosy lip?
   Ask but your heart—it will suggest
   They value not what makes me blest."

Martial.

COME, Chloe, and give me sweet kisses,
   For sweeter, sure, girl never gave;
But why, in the midst of my blisses,
   Do you ask me how many I'd have?
I'm not to be stinted in pleasure,
Then, prithee, my charmer, be kind;

For whilst I love you above measure,
To numbers I'll ne'er be confined.

Count the bees that on Hybla are playing,
    Count the flowers that enamel the fields;
Count the flocks that on Tempe are straying,
    Or the grain that rich Sicily yields;
Go, number the stars in the heaven,
    Count how many sands on the shore;
When so many kisses are given,
    I still shall be craving for more.

To a heart full of love let me hold thee,
    To a heart, which, dear Chloe, is thine!
With my arms I'll for ever enfold thee,
    And twist round thy limbs like a vine.
What joy can be greater than this is?
    My life on thy lips shall be spent;
But the wretch that can number his kisses
    With few will be ever content."

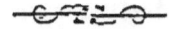

Your Nose.

"How very odd that poets should suppose
 There is no poetry about your nose,
 When, plain as a man's nose upon his face,
 A noseless face would lack poetic grace.
　　Noses have sympathy, a lover knows;
 Noses are always touched when lips are kissing—
 And who would care to kiss if nose were missing?
　　Why, what would be the fragrance of the rose,
 And where would be the mortal means of telling
　　Whether a vile or wholesome odour flows
 Around us, if we own'd no sense of smelling?
　　I know a nose—a nose no other knows—
　　'Neath starry eyes, o'er ruby lips it grows—
 There's beauty in its form and music in its blows!"

From the French.

"While you incline that neck of snow
  To every kiss my lips bestow,
  And in those passion-beaming eyes
  Such inexpressive meaning lies,
  Enraptur'd by the kindling glance,
  My soul dissolves in am'rous trance;
  And on your gently heaving breast
  Exanimate, I sink to rest.
    But when our lips in wanton play,
  So sweetly kiss for kiss repay,
  And from that humid, panting lip
  Such sweets, such balmy dews I sip,
  As bathe the newly op'ning flower
  That blooms in some ambrosial bower.
  'Midst heavenly scenes I seem to rove,
  And taste the nectar'd feasts of Jove."

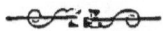

From the Italian.

"The bee sips honey in each flow'ret's bell,
  Thence bearing tempers in her waxen cell;
  Whence man prepares the rich Metheglius juice;
  And gods their sweet nectareous draughts produce.
  But on thy lips hang sweeter dews, my fair,
  Bees seek in flowers, but I find honey there;
  There Venus spreads ambrosia to my taste
  And she alone can yield the sweet repast."

From the German.

"The kiss that you pressed on my lip
    Has but kindled more fiercely the fire,
And e'en gods 'midst their raptures would weep,
    Did they burn as I do with desire.
For scarce had my soul felt the bliss,
    When you left me to mourn that 'twas given;
Is this, to impart the sweet kiss,
    The nectar they boast of in heaven?
No, no—ah! believe me, 'tis merely
    To sharpen the stings of desire,
And make me but feel more severely
    The tortures by which I expire.
So feels, when thirst parches the lip,
    The traveller, to whom rustics tell,
Of the cool, sparkling stream he may sip,
    Yet refuse him access to the well."

"Alas! madame, for stealing a kiss
    Have I so much therein your mind offended?
Or, have I done so grievously amiss
    That by no means can it be e'er amended?
Revenge you, then,—the readiest way is this—
Another give, and see me die with bliss!"

THE END.

www.ingramcontent.com/pod-product-compliance
Lightning Source LLC
Chambersburg PA
CBHW031748230426
43669CB00007B/534